Collaborative
Peer Coaching
That
Improves
Instruction

To our families

Collaborative
Peer Coaching
That
Improves
Instruction

The
2 + 2
Performance Appraisal Model

Dwight W. Allen • Alyce C. LeBlanc

CORWIN PRESS
A Sage Publications Company
Thousand Oaks, California

For information:

Corwin Press
A Sage Publications Company
2455 Teller Road
Thousand Oaks, California 91320
www.corwinpress.com

Sage Publications Ltd.
1 Oliver's Yard
55 City Road
London EC1Y 1SP
United Kingdom

Sage Publications India Pvt. Ltd.
B-42, Panchsheel Enclave
Post Box 4109
New Delhi 110 017 India

Printed in the United States of America

Library of Congress Cataloging-in-Publication Data

Allen, Dwight William.
Collaborative peer coaching that improves instruction: The 2 + 2
performance appraisal model/Dwight W. Allen and Alyce C. LeBlanc.
    p. cm.
Includes index.
ISBN 1-4129-0608-3 (cloth)—ISBN 1-4129-0609-1 (pbk.)
    1. Mentoring in education. 2. Peer review. 3. Teaching teams.
I. Title: 2 + 2 performance appraisal model. II. LeBlanc, Alyce C. III. Title.
LB1731.4.A44 2005
371.14′4—dc22

                                    2004011551

                06 07 10 9 8 7 6 5 4 3 2

Acquisitions Editor:	Kylee Liegl
Editorial Assistant:	Jaime Cuvier
Production Editor:	Melanie Birdsall
Copy Editor:	Cheryl Duksta
Typesetter:	C&M Digitals (P) Ltd.
Proofreader:	Tricia Lawrence
Indexer:	Michael Ferreira
Cover Designer:	Anthony Paular

Contents

Foreword

This is a time in American educational history when it finally has been empirically confirmed that teachers matter. We now know through science what we have always known in our hearts, namely, that what teachers believe and what they do in classrooms make a difference in the lives of our children. New, uncertified teachers do not do as much for our children as do certified teachers from the universities. Experienced teachers do more for our children than do novice teachers. It has been shown that there is an enormous difference in performance between children who have had exemplary teachers for three years and those who've had poor teachers for three years. For students of average ability, the quality of their teacher can determine whether they will attend college. As with all professionals, teachers need to be good at what they do.

But then how do we treat our teachers? With few exceptions, we isolate them from each other, refuse to pay much for their professional development, provide the wrong kinds of professional development, evaluate them in perfunctory or demeaning ways, and in general make the task of teaching so onerous that many of the best and brightest who enter the field leave within the first three to five years. Those who stay often lose their joy of teaching. This is certainly no sensible way to run a profession. But sometimes little things can have a big impact.

The 2 + 2 program described in this volume has characteristics that make it possible to positively impact our teachers and our students, with a minimum investment of time and money. It is clear to me that the 2 + 2 program is worth trying in our schools, and its influence is worth evaluating. We have learned from Asian teachers that lesson study—where groups of teachers regularly visit other teachers and provide feedback on the lessons they observe—is an important part of the professional development of teachers. In fact, it is how Asian teachers learn to teach. America's teachers are not yet engaging in this remarkable approach to teacher development, though we are slowly learning how to do that. But an American version of the Asian style of lesson study seems integral to the 2 + 2 program described in this book. The 2 + 2 program functions as a version of lesson study that is compatible with American school culture and the norms of our teaching profession. Like the Asian version of lesson study, this program provides teachers with a mechanism to receive feedback from peers. It also reduces the isolation of teachers from one another, and it should increase mutuality—the sense that at a particular school site teachers feel that they are in this profession together and that they are teaching so that their students can learn. Any program of staff development that might move us toward these ends should be promoted.

The description of the 2 + 2 program that follows comes from authors who know schools and have experience with the program they promote. They also wrote this book in a descriptive, caselike form, rather than a didactic one, making it very clear to readers. In my professional life, I see few educational ideas and practices that are both simple and rich with possibilities. This, however, is one of those. I hope educators will try and learn from 2 + 2 as they implement it in many and diverse school settings.

—David C. Berliner
Regents' Professor
College of Education
Arizona State University

Prologue

Once there was a land where education was considered a most important priority, yet student performance was unsatisfactory. From "education presidents" to continuous reform efforts to national goals, much time and rhetoric were expended to resolve the problem. The real educational process, though, took place in individual classrooms, between students and teachers everywhere.

In the schools, administrators were deeply concerned and exhorted teachers to produce better results. Experts devised ever more complex appraisal systems. Most required several visits to each classroom by an administrator. Otherwise, though, the administrators remained in their offices most of the time. Managing budgets and paperwork had become a full-time job in itself. When they did conduct performance appraisal observations, specific feedback to improve teacher performance was seldom included. Instead, teachers received ratings in several areas defined as important to good teaching performance.

> Today's world of educational reform is little more than make-believe.

Though rare, it wasn't unheard of for teachers to be rated without a single visit by the administrator since the process was often considered a nuisance and a waste of time. As long as a teacher received a good rating, the process was considered complete. Appraisal systems were often best suited for the rare situation where seriously deficient performance required documentation.

Teachers tried to find ways to improve their students' achievement, too. They attended many conferences, seminars, and courses. But the implementation of conference ideas in the classroom was largely an unsuccessful proposition. Teachers were on their own when it came to implementation and rarely received feedback or follow-up help.

Consequently, teachers never knew for sure how they were doing. Except for the infrequent appraisal visits, no one, including other teachers, ever saw them teach. They never saw their colleagues teach either. It just wasn't done. A curious tradition had developed whereby teachers were isolated in their classrooms. It was called professional autonomy.

Teachers were also extremely busy. They were under pressure from educational leaders to find new ways to engage their students in collaborative group learning and problem-solving experiences, to name just two departures from centuries' old tradition. This was not the stuff of teacher training in college, not a reflection of how schools themselves were organized and administrated, but new strategies that teachers were expected to learn, perform, and continuously refine, despite little or no training. Add that to increasing societal problems, growing student diversity, and professional isolation, and little joy remained in the teaching profession.

The world was rapidly becoming a more complex place. Even small businesses were expanding beyond national boundaries. Global commerce required new ways of communicating and working together. Group efforts requiring interpersonal skills, problem-solving abilities, communication, feedback, and trust seemed necessary to maximize business opportunities. Even more urgently, these skills were needed to address some of the issues threatening the planet, such as the deterioration of the environment, caused largely by people, businesses, and nations acting in isolation.

> In our complex world, people need better ways of communicating and working together.

Eventually, some teachers began to wonder, how can we best address student performance when our own professional development is not optimal? What are other teachers doing? How can we improve?

Uncertainty was rampant. Teachers knew that they didn't have to be sick to get better. But typical performance appraisal systems and staff development models seemed to have serious flaws. Frequent feedback and follow-up was needed. Isolation was a tremendous handicap. This book introduces a unique tool capable of addressing these dilemmas: 2 + 2 for teachers.

Acknowledgments

W e wish to thank the many teachers who have so enthusiastically embraced the idea of 2 + 2 observations and feedback. The idea was first pioneered in Namibia and later in China as a vehicle for staff development. In countries where teacher supervisors often have no more than an eighth-grade education, regular 2 + 2 feedback among peers proved tremendously helpful in improving teacher performance. The PRIME Project, a major whole-school reform partnership between the Norfolk Public Schools and Old Dominion University in Norfolk, Virginia, took the concept further. Participating schools incorporated the 2 + 2 program into their reform agenda, and the Norfolk Public School District provided waivers from the district's teacher performance appraisal process for teachers who participated. This partnership, under the leadership of Dwight Allen and Roy Nichols, superintendent of schools in Norfolk at the time, was an important part of the development of 2 + 2. Many thanks to all the teachers who took part in the program, especially the teachers at Lake Taylor High School and Lake Taylor Middle School. Their honest feedback and unmitigated enthusiasm for 2 + 2 provided much of the impetus for this book.

Our thanks also go to Bob Brinton, superintendent of the Camp Lejeune Department of Defense Domestic Dependent Elementary and Secondary Schools (DDESS). As a former Department of Defense Dependents Schools (DoDDS) principal, Bob pioneered the 2 + 2 program in Wiesbaden, Germany, with remarkable success. Another early adopter is Dale Baird, superintendent of the Brunswick County Schools in Brunswick, Virginia. He is currently implementing the 2 + 2 program in all the district's schools. Each new implementation brings additional insights and possibilities. One consistent result everywhere that 2 + 2 has been introduced thus far has been a real sense of appreciation and enthusiasm on the part of teachers.

Dwight would like to thank his wife, Carole, who remains a valued critic of both concept and manuscript. His son Doug has long been engaged in intensive collaboration on 2 + 2. Doug's experience with the successful application of 2 + 2 in the business sector led to the development of a companion volume to this book, *Formula 2 + 2: The Simple Solution for Successful Coaching.* He has also strengthened and added to the concept as it is now being developed and used in education. And Dwight's many students and colleagues at Old Dominion University have continued to support the concept and its implementation in university courses and in our school partnerships. Special mention is due to Kamilla Bahbahani, Chris Fischer, Jonathan Higgins, Jennifer Kemp Kidd, Han Liu, Patrick O'Shea, Zhongtang Ren, Simon Richmond, Lu Ruiling, Lee Vartanian, and Weiping Wang.

Alyce would like to thank her husband, Bob Brinton, for his many insights into the teacher appraisal process and staff development issues. His experience leading a 2 + 2 implementation provided a rich topic of conversation, and their many discussions brought the value and potential of the 2 + 2 program into sharper focus. One could not wish for a more engaged and insightful colleague! Their children, Cara and Andrew, have grown up hearing about 2 + 2, and Alyce thanks them for their patience and support. Now in high school and college, they also contributed much encouragement and feedback of their own.

Finally, we would especially like to thank Anne Meeks, who enthusiastically endorsed the 2 + 2 concept and ensured that our manuscript was brought to the attention of Corwin Press.

As 2 + 2 continues to grow as a tool of feedback and appraisal in the classroom and in other settings, we hope that the spirit of collegiality that has characterized its development will continue to shape 2 + 2 and enable it to transform the onerous task of teacher evaluation into a joyful and productive source of feedback and improvement.

—*Dwight W. Allen and Alyce C. LeBlanc*
Norfolk, Virginia, and Jacksonville, North Carolina

Corwin Press gratefully acknowledges the contributions of the following reviewers:

Cynthia A. Givens
Facilitator, Education Station
Central High School
Cheyenne, WY

Helane Smith Miller
Assistant Principal
Wilson High School
Washington, DC

David C. Munson
Principal
Meadowlark Elementary
    School
Billings, MT

Karen L. Tichy
Associate Superintendent
    for Instruction
Catholic Education Office
Archdiocese of St. Louis, MO

Introduction

*C*ollaborative *Peer Coaching That Improves Instruction* tells the story of one school's implementation of 2 + 2 for teachers, a collaborative approach to the improvement of teaching and learning. In the narrative, details of the 2 + 2 model gradually emerge as the teacher leaders and principal of John Dewey High School identify problems grounded in systemic processes that encourage teacher isolation and ineffectual staff development. The account, though fictionalized, is based on the experiences of the authors with 2 + 2 implementations in schools. Readers seeking a complete description of the 2 + 2 for teachers model prior to reading the book are referred to the section "2 + 2: Frequently Asked Questions" at the end of the book, following the epilogue. There, readers will find an overview of the 2 + 2 for teachers model as well as a detailed explanation of implementation processes. This section is also valuable for readers who may wish to plan a 2 + 2 implementation after reading the book.

Why is teacher isolation a major catalyst for the development and implementation of a model such as 2 + 2 for teachers? As is widely acknowledged among educators, isolation from other adults is one of the less-heralded hallmarks of the teaching profession. Some teachers view this circumstance positively, as an indicator of professional autonomy. Many, though, readily admit to feelings of uncertainty and discouragement at the lack of professional feedback. How can it be otherwise when it's human nature to learn from external as well as internal feedback? Dedicated professionals have a need to achieve, to grow, and to make progress in their craft. Teachers already exert extra effort and expend long hours to improve student performance. But without the feedback and encouragement necessary for effective

> Isolation from other adults, one of the less-heralded hallmarks of the teaching profession, significantly hinders teacher effectiveness.

guidance, the only option becomes doing the same things harder. More often than not, the result is burnout rather than success or satisfaction.

Teacher performance appraisal is, in most schools, the only avenue for teachers to receive feedback. However, the nature of the typical teacher performance appraisal, with its infrequent observations and emphasis on ratings, makes it an inadequate vehicle for professional development and improvement. Teachers today are challenged to be lifelong learners. But who provides teachers with the encouragement and support needed for continuous learning? Where does the joyful satisfaction of receiving positive feedback and supportive suggestions for improvement come from? Too often, a disconnect exists between joy and learning, between feedback and improvement of instruction, between schools and parents, between teachers and administrators, and among teachers themselves.

We believe there is a way to alleviate isolation, promote professional growth, and reestablish vital connections among teachers. A simple but radical program of feedback known as 2 + 2 for teachers requires no additional funding. Implementing 2 + 2 is feasible even given the daunting time constraints faced by teachers. 2 + 2 for teachers is based on frequent, mutual feedback from peers, students, and administrators. Teachers regularly visit one another's classrooms during instructional time for as long as it takes to write two compliments and two suggestions for improvement. It has already been successfully implemented in several school districts, and, where it has been introduced, feelings of support, trust, wonder, and joy have been awakened.

2 + 2 can't solve every problem and is not a panacea for improved teaching. We believe, however, that it is an important—and doable—step toward the professionalization of teaching. 2 + 2 creates a connection for the ongoing feedback necessary for continuous improvement. Just as important, 2 + 2 is a source of increased meaningful contact and discussion among teachers and a first step toward true collaboration. 2 + 2 allows for administrator participation in a less threatening context than the traditional performance appraisal. Even 2 + 2 feedback from students is valued. In light of our experience with 2 + 2 in schools, we encourage you to keep an open mind as you read about the potential of 2 + 2 to transform teachers. 2 + 2 is simple in concept yet rich in possibilities.

> 2 + 2: A simple, important step toward teacher professionalism.

One of those possibilities is the way 2 + 2 can serve as a powerful performance appraisal alternative. After all, if the purpose of performance appraisal is to improve instruction through feedback on classroom performance, wouldn't frequent 2 + 2 feedback from administrators, teachers, and students serve this purpose quite admirably?

When schools and school districts cannot easily alter their negotiated or mandated teacher performance appraisal programs, 2 + 2 can be implemented very effectively as a supplement to the formal performance appraisal system. The benefits of frequent feedback from a variety of sources will not be lost.

Another possibility is that the practice of 2 + 2 will support a culture of joyful teachers. Why is that of concern? A joyful person, according to the dictionary, is full of joy; is feeling, expressing, or causing joy; or is glad or happy. Joy is a natural condition of learning. Brain research tells us that there is a connection between one's state of mind and one's ability to learn. Brain chemistry influences the quality and speed of learning. Teaching and learning are more successful under joyful conditions, and frequent, supportive feedback can help create those conditions. Small children are naturally joyful learners. Their teachers can be joyful, too.

About the Authors

 **Dwight W. Allen, Ed.D.,** is Eminent Scholar of Educational Reform at Old Dominion University in Norfolk, Virginia. He received his A.B. (with Distinction) in history, with honors in humanities, from Stanford University in Palo Alto, California. He continued at Stanford and completed both his M.A. and his Ed.D. in education.

Dwight is also heavily involved in global concerns and continues to serve, as he has for more than twelve years, as the International Technical Advisor for the United Nations Development Program in China as well as a consultant to the Department of Defense Dependent Schools in Germany. He also serves or has served as a consultant for schools and universities in Zimbabwe, Botswana, Zambia, India, South Africa, Israel, Uganda, Malawi, and Greece.

He is the coauthor (with his son, Douglas B. Allen, Ph.D.) of a companion volume to *Collaborative Peer Coaching That Improves Instruction.* That volume, *Formula 2 + 2: The Simple Solution for Successful Coaching,* is based on the application of the 2 + 2 model in the corporate sector. He is also the coauthor of *American Schools: The 100 Billion Dollar Challenge* (with Bill Cosby, Ph.D.), which was published in electronic format by Time Warner in 2000 and was named one of six nonfiction finalists in the International eBook Awards. In 2002, Dwight was named University Teacher of the Year by the State Council for Higher Education in Virginia, and the University of Massachusetts, Amherst, honored him by establishing the Dwight W. Allen Professorship of Educational Policy and Reform in 2001.

Dwight is known as a leading proponent of reformed educational systems for the future and has written literally scores of influential papers and magazine articles on all aspects of the topic. He is an in-demand speaker and has delivered hundreds of lectures on national and international platforms. He has been the recipient of numerous grants for studies of educational systems.

Dwight is married and has three sons, two daughters, and six grandchildren.

 **Alyce C. LeBlanc, Ph.D.,** is Curriculum Specialist for the School of Education at Capella University. In addition to teaching, she has developed numerous instructor-led graduate courses for Web-based online delivery in the School of Education. Alyce has a particular interest in teacher preparation programs and currently has a lead role in the development of a new master's degree program for K–12 teachers at Capella University.

Alyce initially studied music at Oberlin College in Oberlin, Ohio, and later at the Staatliche Hochschule für Musik, where she graduated with distinction in piano performance. She was a prizewinner in several international piano competitions.

She furthered her studies at the University of Southern California, where she earned an M.S. in Systems Management, later completing her Ph.D. in Urban Services/Education at Old Dominion University. She has subsequently taught at Oberlin College, Old Dominion University, and National-Louis University in Germany. She has been active in teacher preparation programs and school reform issues and has been a consultant to teachers and education leaders in the Czech Republic and China, as well as in the United States. She was awarded a Fulbright Scholarship and was recently presented the Harold Abel Outstanding Faculty Award at Capella University.

Alyce is married and the mother of two teenagers, a daughter and a son.

1

The Performance Appraisal Paradox

Performance appraisal exists to help teachers improve instruction. The categories and domains of the performance appraisal instrument are based on extensive research and break the teaching act into useful, discrete components. School administrators observe staff frequently; give helpful, specific feedback; follow up on suggestions; provide additional assistance; and praise excellence. Teachers thrive on feedback, are motivated to improve, and experience satisfaction through professional growth. The appraisal system is taken seriously and is an integral part of staff development. This, at least, is the intent.

In theory

In practice, however, performance appraisal exists to document marginal teaching performance. Categories and domains are useful in identifying deficiencies. The school administrators observe staff infrequently, give perfunctory "pats on the back" to 90% of teachers, and have no time or opportunity to follow up on any suggestions for improvement. Schoolteachers receive little feedback, are anxious about performance appraisal ratings, and are relieved when the process is complete. The appraisal system is often subverted by cutting corners and has no link to staff development or professional growth.

> The current performance appraisal system does little to help teachers improve.

Andy Armstrong was nervously anticipating his principal's third and final classroom observation of the year. Tall, slender, and bespectacled, Andy was in his late twenties. While the past six years teaching English at John Dewey High had greatly developed his confidence, performance appraisal time inspired a touch of uncertainty. He thought, *I wouldn't mind these visits if only they didn't happen so rarely. Three years of teaching with no one but students in here, and suddenly it's time for the administration to take a look again. Three visits—of just half a class period each!* He wasn't comfortable with the idea that his performance appraisal rating—a permanent part of his personnel file—was based on these three visits. Even his students acted differently when Dr. Cecilia Fusz, the principal, was in the room. Thankfully, Andy had received some advance notice of this last visit.

Not that Dr. Fusz wasn't a good administrator, Andy reflected. She had impressive credentials. As far as he knew, she was truly concerned about the quality of education at Dewey High. He was just not convinced that she understood the realities of front-line, day-to-day teaching—at least not in his department. With her math background, she sometimes seemed out of touch with the significant language problems of these urban students. He, as an English teacher, felt that he had a more accurate understanding of how to address the basics in the language arena.

Still, he hoped Sissy, as Dr. Fusz was known among the staff, would be pleased with what she saw. These performance appraisal observations were his only chance to get feedback on his teaching. Reassurances that he was on the right track were always welcome. Ideally, he'd hear mostly good things at the post-observation conference. It was too late in the year to hear any substantial criticism—too late for him to make changes, that is. Sissy hinted at his last two conferences that he might find it helpful to explore some new teaching strategies, use more variety in his approach. But he wasn't very clear on what that meant. Did she want him to de-emphasize grammar and spelling? Ask more questions? Get rid of worksheets? Would she be looking for something specific today?

Sissy always seemed to have some new idea about how things should be done. At faculty meetings, she often talked about things like creating more relevance for all students and teaching problem-solving skills. She liked the idea of an interdisciplinary approach to teaching. She wasn't completely off track, he conceded to himself. "Relate everything to students' experiences and involve them actively in class," she exhorted. Andy had nothing against any of that, at least not in theory. But the underlying message was that he needed to raise student achievement, a euphemism for raising test scores, as if all teachers weren't trying their best to do just that. Besides, where was the time going to come from to plan interdisciplinary units? Just covering the basics was difficult enough. Being an English teacher usually meant putting in longer hours than most other teachers, given the lengthy writing assignments to grade. Any discretionary time during the day was spent at his desk, grading assignments and planning the next class sessions.

As he leafed through his lecture notes, he began to take stock. *No one can fault my preparation,* he reflected. *And I'm seeing some solid progress. In general, the quality of the written work seems to be improving, and a few of the kids are coming up with some really original ideas. But if I'm teaching so well, why do some of them seem bored and unmotivated? Even some of the best students seem tired and listless by the end of class.* He went back and forth, ruminating. How could he really know just how effective he was? Some days everything worked, but at other times Andy felt like his best-laid plans had somehow become unrecognizable. *Thank goodness the teachers here are friendly and supportive,* he thought. *But it would be great to know how I fit in.*

To Andy, most teachers appeared self-confident and completely in charge. *Nearly everyone complains about the difficulties of teaching, but no one seems to have self-doubt,* he thought. His student teaching days came to mind. *That was probably the last time I really got any input.* He felt a little nostalgic for that time in his life, remembering how motivated and excited he had been. True, he had been concerned about doing well. But the critique and follow-up he received had definitely built up his confidence. *It was invigorating and somehow nonthreatening, too. How times change,* he mused.

> Student teaching: Last chance for real feedback for many teachers.

Andy found himself wondering how Joy, a colleague down the hall, would fare in her performance appraisal this year. A veteran English teacher, she had a stellar reputation throughout the department. She'd always been popular among the students, too. Andy was pleased to have her as a colleague. She'd helped him considerably when he first arrived at Dewey High. Even now, they often had lunch with the same group of teachers. He never trusted himself to ask her—or anyone else—for advice. He often wondered how other teachers would approach a particular topic or what ideas they might have about introducing a controversial book—not that he couldn't do it on his own. But sometimes he got the urge to do something differently and consult with a fellow professional about it. He had long realized that he knew little about how other teachers managed their classrooms. That left him up in the air about how to assess his own abilities as a teacher. Try as he might to tune it out, the idea that he would be compared unfavorably with Joy was a persistent, unpleasant thought.

As time to begin class drew near, Andy couldn't quite shake the feeling that this was a test. Peering out the classroom door he spotted Sissy as she wove a purposeful path down the crowded hall. A large, attractive woman with a businesslike air, she was hard to overlook. He ducked back into the room. If his two most behaviorally challenged students would just relax and keep quiet, he'd be fine. He wondered what the other teachers did to capture their students' interest. On a good day, the rest of the students were more or less manageable. But as his rambunctious third-period students jostled their way through the door, he knew he would have his work cut out for him.

Meanwhile down the hall, Joy was relieved to begin her prep period. She pushed her thick auburn hair away from her face and removed her reading glasses. She was feeling uncharacteristically lethargic. She almost felt that she needed some additional support of some kind. *Is this what burnout feels like?* she wondered to herself. Feelings of discouragement and isolation had taken her by surprise this year. Sure, a lot of socializing went on at the high school during lunch and preparation periods. Most talk centered around the latest faculty meeting, new regs from the district, the new quality initiative, or personal news. But more and more she missed any real dialogue about what was actually happening—and not happening—in the classroom. She was no longer sure how effective her teaching was. Were other teachers feeling the same way?

Joy, with twenty years' teaching experience, was certainly no beginner. She took great pride in giving her best effort, in her reputation as an excellent teacher, and in her high performance appraisal ratings. In addition, she was an active member of the teacher social committee and was often the first to welcome new teachers to Dewey High. Under her wing, they learned the intricacies of supply room procedures and faculty politics and gained moral support along the way. This was strictly an informal effort on her part but one that provided much satisfaction.

Things, though, had definitely changed over the years. At urban high schools like Dewey High, teachers were doing more and, if test scores were to be believed, accomplishing less and less.

New unfamiliar challenges arose daily it seemed. Teaching now was certainly different from teaching at the beginning of her career. Broken families, poverty, mobility, and the rapidly changing world outside had conspired to make school seem irrelevant. And self-control had become more difficult for many of her students. In response, teachers were being asked to change the way they taught; to be sensitive to multicultural issues and different learning styles; to integrate technology and cooperative learning into their classrooms; to offer project-based, interdisciplinary curriculum in collaboration with other teachers; and, of course, to promote higher level thinking skills. The challenges felt overwhelming at times. She wondered how other teachers made all this happen in their classrooms.

Well, she thought, returning to the tasks at hand, *I'd better focus if Sissy is going to observe me this afternoon. No point in raising red flags with the administration.* She felt reasonably comfortable around Sissy, although, apart from the classroom observations and faculty meetings, she rarely saw her. Sissy had already observed her class-room teaching twice this past year and had seemed positive in her post-observation conferences.

Joy settled down as her fourth-period class entered the room. She enjoyed her students when they were ready to learn. But too often these days she felt as if she were just going through the motions. *Never mind,* she thought as Sissy sat down in the back of the classroom, *they are pretty good motions.* She knew she could expect perfunctory compliments from Sissy at the post-observation conference, and, except for the final conference in another month, the

> Veteran teachers don't take today's performance appraisal processes seriously.

performance appraisal exercise would be over for the year. Joy wasn't sure what purpose the whole appraisal process served, but veteran teachers like her didn't take it all that seriously. Aside from a pat on the back, nothing had ever come of it—no salary raises, no promotions, not even any meaningful dialogue about the teaching process—just another distraction in an already stressful schedule. She faced the class, welcomed Sissy, and smiled.

Later in the day, after the students had been dismissed and the teacher parking lot stood nearly empty, Sissy sighed. She wasn't looking forward to another afternoon of paperwork, with the race to meet the teacher evaluation deadline upon her once again. Final performance appraisal conferences with teachers would begin in three weeks, and she hadn't started the written appraisal reports. Somehow the appraisal process seemed irrelevant. Budget projections, parental complaints, dropout rates, test scores, and a new district quality initiative were all much more urgent items on her docket. Those were the things most visible to her supervisors. The completed teacher appraisals were seldom reviewed by anyone. Sissy was not even sure that failure to comply with the performance appraisal system calendar would catch her superiors' attention.

Strategies to improve instruction and to raise student achievement were her real focus, all of which seemed rather removed from the performance appraisal system. As the instructional leader of the school, she was especially interested in reform agendas emphasizing such strategies as instruction across subject areas. She also considered it important to involve the students in defining and solving problems linked to their own experience. She had exhorted her staff time and again in faculty meetings to adopt newer, more interactive teaching methods and was in the process of planning workshops and inservice opportunities for the next school year.

The new ideas seemed to have evoked a foot-dragging response from most of Sissy's faculty, despite her efforts to convince them of the benefits of change. She'd never really received any direct feedback from her teachers about it, but her appraisal observations told her that not much was changing. Some of these teachers were just hopelessly stuck. She had a difficult time understanding their resistance. Perhaps she should simply mandate new assessment strategies or an interdisciplinary unit. *The performance appraisal process is really no help with any of this,* Sissy thought. The appraisal process provided little if any linkage with the professional development of her staff. No wonder it was May before appraisals received her full attention.

"What a time-consuming and thankless exercise," she groaned. "I already know which 95% of my teachers are competent and able. They know it, too. But beyond that, most teachers feel they need to receive a rating higher than 'satisfactory.'"

The fine differences between a proficient, an outstanding, and a satisfactory teacher were supposed to be observable behaviors. She read the descriptions of the behaviors once again. Under the domain "Delivery of Instruction," for example, a proficient teacher was described as one who "consistently and effectively gets students on task quickly and maintains a high level of student time on task throughout the lesson and during transition times." The satisfactory description read "Gets students on task quickly and maintains a high level of student time on task throughout the lesson and during transition times."

The whole process of official appraisal was largely a matter of determining which rating to assign each teacher. But how did she distinguish between teachers who got their students on task during the observation and teachers who did it consistently and effectively? After all, she only observed each teacher three times during the year. If a teacher had his or her students on task during each observation, was that consistent and effective or simply satisfactory? Somehow the objective observable behaviors seemed to require her subjective judgment. The appraisal had seven domains of teaching, each with many subcategories. And how useful was it to try to observe the nearly fifty different subcategories of behaviors under the seven domains? She knew she would be looking at the big picture for most ratings.

True, in the past five years, she'd had to place two less than competent teachers on plans of action—appraisal jargon for instituting procedures with teachers who were in dire need of substantial improvement. Steps necessary to assist such teachers, as well as consequences for failure to improve, were spelled out in detail by the performance appraisal system. This aspect of the appraisal system was actually helpful because it provided Sissy with a means to document deficiencies and enforce remedial procedures. Ironically, the appraisal system really seemed most useful when the performance of especially weak teachers was being assessed.

Sissy briefly considered giving every teacher a satisfactory rating. Much time and effort would be saved because she had to justify in writing any rating above satisfactory in each domain. Certainly there would be no negative professional consequences for the teachers. Every teacher with a satisfactory rating and above was treated the same by the school system. Only when ratings were less than satisfactory did the appraisal system prescribe a series of consequences. Many teachers would be upset, though, if their performance were considered merely satisfactory. She certainly didn't want performance appraisals to dampen morale in an already challenging school. *The teachers' union might have something to say about it too,* she reminded herself.

Getting to the task at hand, Sissy pulled Andy's folder and reviewed her notes of that day's observation. Andy was a very capable teacher who knew his curriculum well. The better students seemed to respect him, and his lectures were interesting and relevant. But Sissy did wish he had better classroom management skills. Maybe he should do a little less lecturing; his approach seemed so outdated.

Then there was the drill work (on parts of speech) that was downright tedious. She realized she had come to the same conclusion three years ago during his last appraisal. At that time, when she suggested a more interactive approach, he hinted that English was different from math, but he said he'd give it a try. With no opportunity to follow up on it, though, Sissy hesitated to mention it at all this time. So much for staff development! Of course, Andy was a clear asset to the school. He was the ninth-grade class sponsor and ran a drama club after school. But she did feel obligated to remind him to vary his teaching styles. Perhaps she could give him the second highest rating.

Traditional Performance Appraisal

- Is time-consuming
- Provides infrequent feedback
- May negatively affect morale
- Frequently causes anxiety
- Is useful only for teachers with serious weaknesses
- Has neither consequences nor rewards for competent teachers
- Does not provide for follow-up
- Cannot be objective
- Provides no link to staff development
- Is usually not an instrument of professional growth
- Is often not taken seriously by the administrator or the teacher

---

As Sissy pondered her options, her eyes fell on the notes she'd taken during Joy's classroom observation. Joy was one of those teachers who seemed to be respected by the entire faculty. Joy certainly had unique talents. She was a well-versed veteran and could practically teach in her sleep. She had great rapport with her students, was always well prepared, and stayed in touch with parents. Her work with novice teachers was a great asset, too. Sissy hesitated. Was it her imagination that Joy seemed to be less engaged this year? Joy appeared to be satisfied with simple answers, and her comments were a bit perfunctory. She had seen Joy teach differently during the last appraisal cycle, though, where Joy had facilitated some really exciting discussions. Had she caught Joy on the wrong day this time? If she mentioned it, would Joy be typical of so many teachers who felt demoralized if she offered suggestions for improvement? Did being an excellent teacher mean there was no room for further improvement?

Sissy frowned, feeling a little frustrated. Her classroom observations were so few and far between that she could only see enough to reassure herself that most teachers were reasonably capable. A few observations also sufficed to identify those who weren't doing well. And she could only really engage in follow-up activities with the most marginal of teachers. The business of writing up performance appraisals for good teachers seemed to be just an exercise in giving recognition for a job well done. Giving recognition was important, of course, but it was just a small part of staff development. Outside, she noticed the sounds of soccer practice fade away. Six o'clock! She realized she had been dwelling on the appraisal issue for far too long. Trying to mold performance appraisal into a vehicle for staff development simply wasn't going to work. As she quickly reached for her computer keyboard, she had only one thought: *Let's get this over with!*

The pace of the school year accelerated predictably as May gave way to June. Teacher performance appraisal conferences were sandwiched between finals, grading, special events, parties, and endless year-end paperwork. Most teachers and students had their sights set on the final day of school.

Sissy remained concerned about student achievement levels. The school district had indicated at various times during the past year that the newly developed state standards were going to have important consequences. Everyone was still unsure about what that meant, but no one doubted that standardized tests would remain the performance measure of choice.

More than that, though, Sissy wanted to produce better outcomes for students in ways that standardized tests didn't measure. Sissy thought that the students would benefit from a more integrated approach to a variety of subject areas. She wanted the students to be involved in issues that were important to them, issues that were connected to their lives outside of school. She also believed that the students would learn better from teachers

> Administrators are as frustrated as teachers with current practices of performance appraisal.

who were learning and growing as professionals. So, after much thought, she mandated interdisciplinary units for the entire faculty. As a first step, each teacher was required to develop and teach at least one interdisciplinary unit the following year. Not ideal staff development, she was sure, but given the lack of time and resources it was the best she could do.

Andy's conference had been conducted at the beginning of June. He was satisfied with his appraisal rating but was confused by the comments about his teaching style. Sissy probably just didn't realize the difficulties he faced, and she certainly knew little about teaching English. He already felt overworked. Even if he knew how to change, how would he know when he'd improved? Too bad she hadn't said something about it at the beginning of the year when he might have been able to work on it for her next observation. It was discouraging to discover that she found his efforts lacking. The new requirement for interdisciplinary teaching also worried him. What did it mean for him? Very little was said about any training or support for teachers. Then again, who could tell how, or even if, Sissy would follow up on it next year?

On the last day of teacher duty that school year, Andy packed up and checked out of school, visibly relieved that the year was over. He felt genuinely in need of time away from school to refuel his energy. Nonetheless, he hadn't lost his desire to teach. On the contrary, he resolved to work hard to improve the next year, even without knowing exactly how to go about it.

Joy was also in her own world as she left the building on the last day of school. She had had a reasonably good year and had been deemed exceptional (the equivalent of an *A* grade) in all of the major teaching domains of her appraisal. Yet, sad to say, she felt a little frustrated about being a teacher. She was certain something was missing. The principal had said only good things about her teaching at the final conference. Still, there hadn't been time for any reflection or discussion, so how could she really know how she was doing?

Even more worrisome, where had all the fun gone? She was sure she could manage an interdisciplinary unit. But she knew that many of her colleagues were concerned and felt unsupported. Morale was sagging at Dewey High at a time when the students needed more attention than ever.

Sissy was equally disheartened as summer vacation began. She felt that even though her faculty was as devoted a group of teachers as could be found anywhere, yet another year had come and gone without any tangible sign of change. *Just getting through the year is success enough in an urban school,* she thought. But the real heart of education was, of course, the classroom teacher, and helping teachers grow professionally seemed somehow beyond her abilities. She had no illusions about changing very much through her interdisciplinary mandate, but she felt she had to begin exercising instructional leadership in a visible way. Unfortunately, an adversarial tone to faculty–administration relations was developing, and it threatened to dampen whatever progress they were making.

Joy, Andy, Sissy, and indeed the entire faculty had something in common as they began summer vacation—a desire to improve the quality of teaching at Dewey High. But, sadly, no one had the time or the means to do so. Although they had all survived another year, and despite sustained individual efforts and small victories here and there, joylessness reigned.

2

The Fine Art
of Feedback

An Interlude

*It is the supreme art of the teacher to awaken joy in creative
expression and knowledge.*

—Albert Einstein (1879–1955)

Joy was still preoccupied with thoughts of her lackluster school year
when she received a call from an old friend. Zelda, a performing
artist and former classmate, was now a professor at a nearby university. Joy was delighted to hear from Zelda, and they agreed to meet
for lunch the next week. *How fortuitous*, Joy thought. *Zelda always has
a fresh perspective on any number of things.*

The following Monday, Joy was first to arrive at their rendezvous
at a Chinese restaurant. She soon caught sight of Zelda hurrying
across the parking lot. Smiling to herself, Joy noted the petite, youth-
ful figure with wavy red hair escaping in every direction. Zelda was
definitely the same old bundle of energy!

"I have to tell you, Joy, it's been an exciting morning," Zelda
began after they had exchanged greetings. "We're hosting a guest artist
who's here on tour. His master class this morning was extraordinary.

And this afternoon he's going to coach our trio. With a new program to perform in a couple of weeks, we're glad for the chance to get some feedback. Sometimes we're so focused on getting every detail right, that we're in danger of missing the big picture."

"That sounds wonderful," Joy responded. "What a great opportunity! But aren't you a little nervous? I mean, you're the professor! Aren't you the one who does the teaching? What will your students think, let alone your colleagues?" Joy hesitated. "I guess I'm just a little surprised."

"You know," Zelda said lightly, "it's part of the routine for musicians to listen to each other formally and informally. When someone gives me feedback, I don't necessarily agree with all of it. But I always get another perspective on my musical interpretation, and I get some great ideas to experiment with, too. You can't hear everything yourself! When someone else is listening, I usually focus differently on what I'm doing. And I always learn something when I'm asked to listen to someone else."

Zelda thought for a moment, then gestured dramatically. "We have to be very free with our opinions! We're like a team working to achieve a common goal. Everyone trusts one another because everyone wants the final product to be the best it can be. I know this isn't exactly like your work, but don't you ever want to see what other teachers are doing in their classrooms?"

| Feedback gives everyone new perspectives. |

Joy searched for the right words. "You do seem to have a great way of getting real feedback and sharing ideas on what you're doing," she replied. "But teaching is different. I believe teaching is an art, too. But it's really a private performance between the teacher and the students. I guess visiting other classrooms would be a way to get some perspective, but it just isn't done." As she talked, Joy brought Zelda up-to-date on the busy year she'd had. She also couldn't help mentioning her feelings of isolation. "I can't figure out why I feel so discouraged after all these years as a successful teacher," she sighed.

"Well," Zelda replied energetically, "from my perspective it's not very surprising at all. In at least one way, teaching is no different than any other profession: It's impossible to be your best in isolation. Is there no such thing as collaboration among teachers? Peer communication and support? Dialogue? You've got to have feedback! It's essential to improving performance and staying motivated—feedback that is focused, specific, and frequent."

| It's impossible to be your best in isolation. |

Zelda, never at a loss for words, warmed to her topic. "Can you imagine a golfer never seeing other golfers play? Or never gaining feedback on his or her own game from another professional? How about a lawyer never seeing another lawyer in court? Or a surgeon never seeing an operation performed? Or never being coached while practicing a new procedure? How would anyone improve without feedback? Wouldn't that lead to stagnation? What a total dead end! It certainly seems to me that so little interaction would keep a profession as a whole from reaching higher levels of competence."

Joy smiled at the thought of golfers never seeing anyone else play, or musicians never hearing other musicians, or surgeons never observing a new procedure. What if they were never given feedback? A golfer who was never coached would have a real handicap. Would each surgeon have to try every new procedure on his or her own? Wouldn't it be better if those trained in certain areas could help those who weren't? Or if, at least, there was ample practice-related communication among professionals? Otherwise, how could the medical profession move forward as a whole?

"You see," Zelda continued, "each professional contributes his or her own new ideas to the collective level of expertise in the profession. When a surgeon introduces a new procedure or treatment and the results are positive, the new information is shared. Others are trained. If the innovation withstands the test of time and is adopted by most other doctors, the level of collective expertise in the profession progresses."

"What does that mean for teaching?" Joy wondered aloud. "Are you saying the collective level of teaching practice suffers because so little sharing and consultation goes on among teachers?" She had always known that teachers were essentially on their own. But now Joy saw for the first time a possible downside to that traditional autonomy.

> The collective level of teaching practice cannot improve until better ways are found for teachers to learn from one another.

Zelda pursued her point. "I'm not sure I would go that far, although it would be a logical conclusion. But it seems strange to me that teachers have only themselves and their students as resources for new ideas—although I guess you do have the occasional workshop. But I would have thought your fellow teachers would be the best source of ideas about what works well in the classroom. And how do you support each other as you implement ideas you get from workshops or seminars if there's no feedback on your performance? Isn't there a performance appraisal system?"

"It's not as simple as it seems, Zelda," Joy replied. "I haven't really given it much thought until now, but personally I think it would be great to be able to see what other teachers are doing. I hear of so many good things that teachers could be sharing with each other. The reality is that ideas from workshops usually aren't implemented in the classroom because teachers are left alone to work out the glitches. It's hard to know what's working and what's not when there's no one to advise or observe you. The performance appraisal system is pretty perfunctory, at least if you're not a total disaster. And it doesn't really begin to address how to make the kind of continuous improvement you're suggesting. Schools just aren't set up for teachers to go wandering into other classrooms, either. Some teachers would feel threatened and would resist the idea of another teacher actually watching them teach."

"I guess you mean that the typical culture in schools doesn't really encourage teachers to learn from each other," Zelda elaborated, "but encourages isolation instead. Consider this: Your malaise may be the result of a lack of encouragement and constructive feedback to help keep you interested in improving. You know, the word *encouragement* comes from the word *courage*—to take heart. And you certainly seem disheartened to me."

Encourage

To inspire with hope, courage, or confidence

To give support to; foster

To stimulate; hearten

"You're right. I've lost some of the passion for teaching, which worries me a lot," Joy admitted. "It's not easy to be motivated when you're not sure what to do to improve. You even lose sight of what you're doing well when there's no feedback. A vacuum isn't the best atmosphere for encouragement. So I guess *discouraged* is the appropriate word."

"Maybe there's something that could be done about the isolation you teachers experience," Zelda said thoughtfully. "I read recently about something called 2 + 2 for Teachers. It's about getting teachers out of their own classrooms and into other teachers' classrooms on a regular basis, so they can give each other feedback, in the form of encouragement and suggestions. Our old prof, Dr. James, is giving a 2 + 2 workshop for teachers and administrators this summer. Why don't you check it out? It can't hurt, and it sounds like a lot of fun."

"I don't know how yet another workshop will help, but I'll give it some thought," Joy promised. Fun was something Joy hadn't had in some time. Besides, Dr. James had been one of her favorite professors.

"I hope you didn't mind my suggestion," Zelda remarked as they were about to part company. "But I know you've always inspired your students, so I couldn't help but give you my two cents!"

Joy didn't mind. On the contrary, she felt rather encouraged.

3

What Is 2 + 2 Anyway?

All waste [in education] is due to isolation.

—John Dewey (1859–1952)

Two weeks later, Joy approached the classroom where Dr. James was scheduled to give a talk titled "An Introduction to 2 + 2 for Teachers." After picking up a handout—"2 + 2: The Basic Protocol"— she took a seat near the front of the university classroom. She was joined by about thirty or so teachers and administrators from several schools in the surrounding area.

2 + 2: A Demonstration

"I think the 2 + 2 concept will be easiest to grasp if we begin by conducting a demonstration lesson," Dr. James began. "So I've asked Cara Leigh from Parkgrove Middle School to share a little science with you." Dr. James, a large, white-haired man, then took a seat off to the side to observe. For her demonstration, Cara set up a small experiment in the front of the room involving a glass, a spoon, a fork, and a toothpick.

As she began, she interlaced the tines of the fork with the curved surface of the spoon, so they were stuck solidly together. "Let's pretend this is a science class in which we are studying different

forces. Now, how many of you think I can balance this silverware—it's stainless steel, by the way—on the wooden toothpick and then balance the toothpick on the rim of the glass so that only the toothpick comes in contact with the rim?" Most teachers thought that there was some trick involved and hedged their guesses. *It certainly looks impossible,* Joy thought to herself.

Cara wedged one end of the toothpick between two of the fork's tines and then balanced the toothpick on the rim of the glass. The silverware did not touch the glass but straddled the end of the toothpick. The toothpick itself extended beyond the outside edge of the glass.

"That really looks physically impossible," said one of the teachers, "but I see it with my own eyes. How does it work?"

"If you can wait just a minute," Cara replied, "I'm not quite finished." She then lit the end of the toothpick that was inside the glass with a match. The toothpick burned until it reached the rim of the glass where it extinguished itself. The remainder of the toothpick, with the silverware still firmly attached, was suspended at a ninety-degree angle to the glass. The silverware itself did not come into contact with the glass. Cara's audience was definitely impressed and amused.

"I imagine you're probably asking yourselves a few questions right now," continued Cara. "For example, why did the burning toothpick extinguish itself when it reached the rim of the glass? What forces are working on the toothpick to keep it balanced horizontally across the glass rim? Let me explain. As you can

see, the fork and spoon do not form a right angle to the toothpick but are almost on their sides, angling back toward the glass from the match. From this position they are exerting torque on the toothpick, which keeps the toothpick pressing onto the glass at its pivot point where it meets the glass. Once this torque is exerted, allowing the toothpick and silverware to balance on the pivot point, it does not matter how far the toothpick extends in either direction. When it burns, though, it is extinguished at the glass because the glass absorbs the heat of the flame. This causes the temperature to drop below the toothpick's kindling point. Easy, isn't it?"

"Thank you, Cara," said Dr. James. "Normally, when Cara presents this lesson to her class, she receives a positive response. Yet she really would like to know what would make it even better. Or perhaps she'd like to vary it from time to time. Until now, she's had to rely entirely on her own inspiration. Here's where you come in. I'm going to ask each of you to reflect on the demonstration we just observed. What two compliments about the demo can you give Cara? What two suggestions for improvement can you make? Specific compliments and suggestions are most useful. Please take time now to write two compliments and two suggestions, and we'll share them in a moment."

> Excellent teachers are always trying to make successful lessons even better.

The room quieted as everyone focused on their written feedback. Joy thought it would be difficult to actually provide specific feedback, yet she identified the ideas she wanted to share rather quickly. She was pleased to find she had an easily accessible reservoir of experience to draw on. Within a few minutes, the teachers had passed their 2 + 2 feedback to Cara.

"Let's share some of your comments," suggested Dr. James.

Cara quickly scanned the 2 + 2 sheets and read a few of the compliments.

"Great idea to actually demonstrate the principle."

"I liked the way you used a few common household items to do the activity."

"You really got our attention by doing the demonstration first and the explanation afterwards."

The suggestions were varied. Someone wrote, "You might let the students set up the experiment in groups of three or four, so they can do it themselves."

"Why not let the students gather around the table, so everyone can get a good look?"

"Have you tried stating the objectives for the experiment in advance?"

"What if you asked the students to explain the principles involved and then give them any help they need in finding answers?"

"I think you get the idea," said Dr. James. "Clearly this lesson could be modified in a number of ways. The feedback is specific, simple, and relevant. Cara may even want to try some of your suggestions next time. But if she feels that a suggestion is not relevant or interesting, she is entirely free to disregard it. The important thing is that she now has information from observers about her lesson that she did not have before. She is encouraged that her teaching is successful, and she now has feedback about other ways to approach it. The premise of the 2 + 2 program is simply this: No lesson is so perfect that there is no room for improvement or variation, and no lesson is so poor that there is nothing good to say about it."

> Effective suggestions—feedback for improvement—are usually simple.

"The 2 + 2 for Teachers program is also a simple proposition. Teachers visit each other's classrooms on a routine, frequent basis. Two compliments and two suggestions, in written form, are the result of each visit. Frequent feedback is key. Administrators and students also have a role in 2 + 2. But first, let's look at why 2 + 2 is not only useful but urgently needed."

2 + 2: The Rationale

"This is a simple 2 + 2 equation," said Dr. James as he turned on the multimedia projector. "Please consider the implications of this chart as we talk about why 2 + 2 can make a difference in a teacher's—and, by extension, in a school's—effectiveness."

"If you think about it," Dr. James continued, "you may notice that the first four characteristics—feedback, growth, joy, and trust—are really positive forces opposing the bottom four characteristics—isolation, stagnation, discouragement, and uncertainty. Feedback counteracts isolation, growth opposes stagnation, joy counters discouragement, and trust replaces uncertainty. Let's start by examining the crucial role of feedback in contributing to professional development and, ultimately, a teacher's effectiveness.

"Sometimes it's easy to forget just how important feedback is." Dr. James warmed to his topic and began pacing the room. "Learning simply can't happen without feedback. Now, good teachers know this, of course, and they work to give their students as much feedback as possible. We know that positive feedback, or encouragement, is as important as corrective feedback. We also know that the most useful feedback is specific and timely, rather than global and tardy. Imagine for a moment where your students would be if you never let them know whether they were doing well or poorly, never corrected even simple mistakes, never returned their papers or tests, never answered their questions, and never provided encouragement.

2 + 2 for Teachers: A Special Equation

2 + 2 promotes at least 4 characteristics of an effective teaching staff:

  Feedback

  Growth

  Joy

  Trust

2 + 2 remedies at least 4 problems that limit the effectiveness of a teaching staff:

  Isolation

  Stagnation

  Discouragement

  Uncertainty

"Furthermore," he continued, "imagine the impact if students could not work together, ask a question, listen to each other, or consult in any way. At the end of the course, they would simply receive their grade, too late for them to improve their performance. And isn't a letter grade by itself relatively uninformative? How would they know, specifically, what they needed to do to improve? Naturally," he said, standing still for a moment, "no one here—nor any responsible educator—would advocate that approach to learning.

"Teaching is a profession where continuous learning is also absolutely necessary. I imagine you are all actively involved in staying current with your subject areas or learning about new teaching methods." Teachers nodded their agreement. "I'm sure your professional development also includes things like new programs designed to help students from disadvantaged areas or programs to encourage parental involvement." Again they nodded.

"Good. So you have acquired this new knowledge from courses or workshops. If you took a course for credit, you probably also received some feedback in the form of a grade that reflected how well you learned the material. But isn't there another kind of learning that is very important to every teacher? Indeed, we haven't yet addressed the most important question: How well are you doing in the classroom? What have you learned about your own teaching, and is that knowledge adequate for optimal professional growth? Is there any way to know more? How do you know what kind of teaching is going on in the rest of the profession or even in the rest of the school building? What kind of teacher are you? You see, this is the type of learning that teachers are expected to accomplish with very little feedback."

Dr. James resumed his pacing as a murmur of assent ran through the group. "Think again about the example of the students who were given no specific feedback, guidance, or encouragement from you all year. No one would expect high achievement to be the norm under those circumstances. Learning, in fact, would be quite a joyless undertaking. But what is learning—or developing professionally—like for teachers?

"What if teachers liked a new idea they had seen in a book or workshop but had no one to consult on its implementation? What if teachers had to identify and correct all of their own weaknesses themselves and possibly remain unaware of some element of their teaching that worked to sabotage their success? What if teachers who have experimented successfully with a new strategy kept that knowledge to themselves? What if the teaching profession had an unwritten code that said asking another teacher for help was a sign of weakness? What if that same professional code discouraged teachers from observing other teachers teach?"

Whispers arose from the audience. "It sounds like we're into familiar territory," Dr. James said, smiling. "And it doesn't sound like much fun at all! Does anyone care to comment?"

A teacher near the front of the room raised his hand. "I see your point that teachers don't have much contact with one another, but you almost make it sound as though teachers do everything they can to avoid each other, Dr. James. I can't imagine that's true. The truth is, there's no time for sharing other than during our lunch hour. Teachers are professionals. As professionals, we're always trying to find better ways to reach students. I know my students well, and I do what I feel will best promote their performance.

> No time for sharing: The myth that perpetuates teacher isolation.

"Teachers need to have full autonomy as they teach and interact in the classroom. It's difficult to imagine someone walking in and being able to know all the complexities of a particular teaching situation. Besides, we already get feedback through the performance appraisal process—which has proven to be a big time waster, I might add. I believe any experienced professional can get plenty of feedback by seeing how well his students perform. Peer observation, if that's what you're getting at, would be okay, but I definitely couldn't give it high priority."

His words clearly resonated with a number of the teachers who were present. Dr. James thanked him and then said, "I agree with you, for the most part. Feedback from student performance is invaluable, and certainly the typical teacher performance appraisal is of limited usefulness at best. Teachers, as professionals, make hundreds of instructional decisions every day, and that is as it should be. I know that teachers work hard to make the best choices they can. But let's be careful not to confuse autonomy with isolation. Exercising professional judgment about teaching strategies is one thing, but to insulate oneself from external feedback about teaching performance is something different. We might call it professional isolation.

"Some of you may be old enough to remember Hubert Humphrey who once said, 'National isolation breeds national neurosis.' Does teacher isolation lead to such symptoms of neurosis as insecurity, anxiety, and depression? I don't know. I do know that teacher isolation can lead to teacher uncertainty. When teachers have no firsthand experience of what other teachers in their building are doing, not to mention what a high level of teaching expertise across subject areas and grade levels looks like, they can become uncertain about how well they fit into the profession. Research indicates this may have serious consequences for a teacher's confidence in being able to influence students' success. That is, uncertainty may negatively impact teacher efficacy and thereby undermine student achievement."

> Teacher isolation is an important factor in producing teacher uncertainty and, by extension, undermining student achievement.

As she listened, Joy felt she intuitively understood the effects of isolation. She was experiencing them herself! She also knew that many teachers were not even aware that a problem existed. For years she thought the professional thing to do was to keep most communication with her colleagues on a general or social level. And the best thing she could do for her students was to retreat to her room and keep up with the stacks of written work she'd assigned. She wondered now if this was a viable long-term strategy or if something, indeed, was missing.

"Uncertainty is also a cause of additional stress for teachers," Dr. James went on. "And what teacher needs more stress? We all know that chronic stress can lead to a variety of physical ailments like headaches, digestive problems, or immune system deficiencies. But chronic stress can also affect your brain chemistry in ways that can result in feelings of discouragement or failure. If high levels of cortisol, triggered by chronic stress, are sustained over time, learning and memory can be negatively affected. Even a short-term rise in cortisol levels in the brain can impair your ability to prioritize. To state the obvious, our brains are really our greatest assets in the business of teaching and learning. Trying to teach or learn with a chronically stressed brain is more than unpleasant; it's a real handicap—one that has not been adequately recognized. Recent brain research indicates that our emotional state is far more important to memory and learning that we previously thought. This is true both for students *and* their teachers."

Uncertainty does cause stress, Joy reflected, *and it's a vicious cycle. The more stress, the more uncertainty, and the more uncertainty, the more stress.* She was briefly lost in her own thoughts but quickly returned her attention to Dr. James.

"Clearly, chronic stress and the ensuing high levels of cortisol contribute to difficulty in learning," Dr. James said, "making everyone's job harder. But there is good news as well. Chemicals called endorphins have a positive effect on the brain's capacity to learn. Those of you who exercise regularly may be familiar with the feeling of semieuphoria that can follow an exercise session. The release of endorphins in the brain causes that feeling. Endorphins make us feel good about ourselves and leave us open to learning and problem solving. Teachers and students may not be able to exercise vigorously prior to every class, but, fortunately, there are other triggers for endorphins. Among these triggers is positive social contact, including support and encouragement from people we trust. So creating a supportive and encouraging atmosphere in our classrooms becomes almost essential in providing the best educational environment for our students. This is why I'm a big advocate of joy in the classroom—and of joyful teachers.

"Are there any questions so far?" Dr. James asked. "You look puzzled," he said, gesturing toward a teacher in the first row.

"I'm just thinking about the expectation that teachers would be joyful," the teacher responded. "I think the term *joyful* might be a bit exaggerated, but are you saying that isolation is what keeps teachers from being joyful?"

"Yes, I do see a relationship between isolation and discouragement and between professional dialogue and joy, and I don't find it a bit exaggerated," Dr. James replied. "In the same way that successful teachers build personal relationships with students, support and encouragement of colleagues also involves building personal relationships with one another. I'm sure you do this already to some extent.

"But having friendly and caring colleagues, important as that may be, is just the first step toward professional growth. The question is, how can we get—and give—*professional* support and encouragement? This is actually what 2 + 2 is all about. Professional support and encouragement can spell an end to professional isolation. The 2 + 2 process means opening yourselves to feedback about what is actually happening in your classroom and being willing to share your observations when you visit another classroom. It's a matter of cultivating mutual trust. But the spirit of collaboration that can develop will both enhance professional development and lead to greater personal satisfaction and joy. Joy is simply a feeling of happiness or delight. Is that too much to expect?"

Dr. James acknowledged a teacher who had raised her hand. "Dr. James, I agree that it would be nice to have more dialogue with other teachers on a professional level, but where will the time come from to do 2 + 2 observations? There's never enough time as it is to get everything done as well as we'd like. And if you spent any time inside our school, you'd see that there's not much to be joyful about, either." A few chuckles of agreement followed.

"I certainly believe," Dr. James explained, "that teachers spend time alone grading papers, planning lessons, and attending to a myriad of clerical tasks because they are convinced they are best serving their students that way. After all, there never seems to be enough time. Teachers are among the most dedicated of all professionals, and some focus every available moment on catching up on all their work. Unfortunately, this well-intentioned, short-term strategy will not serve students well in the long term. A teacher who is isolated from professional dialogue has certain limitations. As we've discussed, teachers and the teaching profession cannot develop in a vacuum. With isolation comes stagnation." He paused. "Wouldn't you agree that removing this limitation is in the students' best interest?"

Teachers murmured their agreement. "I never thought about it that way," one teacher conceded, "but I don't know where I'd find the time. Just thinking about it is a little stressful!"

"I'm well aware," Dr. James continued, "that time pressure is a problem not likely to be resolved in the near future. Part of the process of finding time is setting priorities. My suggestion is this: If time is inadequate for teachers to finish their work anyway, why not consider a strategy that will bring long-term results? Frequent feedback continuously introduces new information into the mix, creates fresh perspectives, and stimulates new ideas. Isolation, on the other hand, is neither particularly joyous nor fruitful. And I'm not sure it takes more time to be joyful than to be deadly driven. Joyful can be focused, and joyful can be serious. Joyful can also be playful, and play is a lighthearted way to do some serious learning. 2 + 2 takes very little time—we'll get to just how little time it takes in a moment. I believe the time set aside for 2 + 2 is more than offset by frequent feedback, enhanced perspectives on teaching, and the development of a collaborative school culture."

"Before I continue, are there any other comments?" Dr. James asked. In response, a thoughtful silence filled the room.

> The time spent engaging in 2 + 2 observations is an investment in building a collaborative school culture.

Then a teacher from the back of the room spoke up. "I think we get it as far as the theory goes. My question is, how does it look in practice?"

"I agree," said another teacher. "Can you give us an example of how the 2 + 2 program would work in a school?"

2 + 2: The Implementation

"Okay, let's talk about how 2 + 2 looks in practice. I have here a sample 2 + 2 observation form, which I'll distribute as I talk," said Dr. James as he reached for the handouts on the desk. "Here's how it works. Each teacher takes ten or fifteen minutes to visit another teacher's classroom. While there, the teacher notes two compliments and two suggestions for improvement on a 2 + 2 form. The form should be in duplicate or triplicate so that both the observer and the observed teacher can keep a copy in a 2 + 2 portfolio. When the comments have been written, the observer leaves. Of course, the observer may stay as long as he or she wishes, but the average visit need not be lengthy. Each teacher schedules an average of one observation per week throughout the year. That's all there is to it, except that now each of you will have at least seventy-two compliments and seventy-two suggestions from your colleagues. That's a lot of perspective and encouragement. Incidentally, 2 + 2 can be a very flexible feedback tool. Administrators and supervisors, as well as your students, are other sources of valuable 2 + 2 feedback.

"You'll also see a Reflections section on the form," Dr. James continued. "The observer may write additional comments or reflections here. Or, when you receive your written comments, you may choose to use that space to note your reaction to the feedback or your intention to implement a suggestion. You might also comment afterwards on how implementing a suggestion did or didn't help. This could be valuable information for you to review during the year as you plan your lessons."

Everyone took a moment to review the 2 + 2 form. "Any questions so far?" asked Dr. James.

"I think it's a good idea, but how can I expect teachers to allow me into their classrooms?" was one question.

"I would love to see other teachers and have them observe me, but can I give feedback that doesn't alienate me from my colleagues?" another teacher wanted to know.

"I'm glad you've raised these concerns," Dr. James responded. "Many teachers feel as you do in that they would welcome 2 + 2 feedback and would be very interested in seeing others teach. But since it's simply not done, no one talks about it. After all, most of you have never expressed to your colleagues an interest in having a fellow teacher observe your classroom. But, in fact, 2 + 2 already has been successfully implemented in many schools on a voluntary basis.

"I see no reason for worries about alienation. Don't forget that half of the feedback is strictly positive. In my experience, most people enjoy giving and receiving compliments! But this doesn't mean that the suggestions are necessarily negative. You are providing colleagues with suggestions for improvement, including alternative ideas for a particular lesson. That's valuable feedback! A certain amount of mutual trust in each other's good intentions is taken for granted. Remember to make your comments as specific as possible. As you gain experience with this tool, it will be easier for you to make suggestions for improvement. You'll find that the process sharpens your powers of observation, too."

> More and better feedback: The simple goal of 2 + 2.
>
> 2 + 2 is easy to understand and easy to try.

"I'm enjoying the discussion," a teacher said with enthusiasm. "This is a great idea in theory, and I understand the rationale behind making the effort to observe. I just find it hard to imagine everyone finding time to do this. Some others have already asked about time, and I would be interested in hearing your suggestions."

"I won't argue that there is far too little time allotted for preparation and staff development," Dr. James agreed. "Until schools change their thinking on this, there will be no easy answers. In my experience, once teachers begin the process, finding time tends to become less of an issue. You'll find the total amount of time invested in 2 + 2 is fairly minimal. Perhaps the simplest solution at the moment would be to use your planning time to invest fifteen minutes per week in 2 + 2 observations over the course of a semester. Then you can judge whether it has the potential to enhance your professional growth in substantive ways in the long run. You may be surprised to find that

2 + 2 becomes a priority rather than one more thing to add to your schedules. Alternatively, administrators have hired substitute teachers now and again to help their staff find time for 2 + 2, especially during the beginning stages of implementation.

"Does anyone else have a question before we conclude this session?" he asked.

There were no further questions.

"Our time is up," Dr. James acknowledged. "In conclusion, I truly believe the 2 + 2 concept can be very liberating for teachers. If 2 + 2 sounds intriguing, I encourage you to try it out. Start a program together with a few colleagues. If you are interested in establishing a 2 + 2 schoolwide program, or if you have further concerns or questions, I would be more than happy to discuss it with you.

"For now, let me leave you with this thought: Good news or bad news is useful feedback, but what's often worse than negative feedback is no news, no information at all. And that's where most teachers live, in the No News Zone. The No News Zone produces much uncertainty, no joy, and it makes professional growth very difficult. In contrast, if there's any doubt that teachers feel they've gained something from 2 + 2, please have a look at their own comments." Before he concluded his presentation, Dr. James distributed a handout with initial feedback he'd received from teachers in a pilot school participating in the 2 + 2 program. "Thank you for your interest in 2 + 2," he said, and when he had returned to the front of the room he added, "Before you leave, would you please complete a 2 + 2 form on my presentation this morning?"

The room began to buzz as the session broke up. Joy had thoroughly enjoyed the presentation and noted that teachers truly seemed interested in discussing the notion of peer observation. She began to browse through some of the teachers' comments that Dr. James had distributed. *Hmm*, she mused, *maybe it's time to get out of my little box*. She determined then and there to see what she could do to bring 2 + 2 to Dewey High.

2 + 2: A First Step

Over the next couple of weeks, Joy continued to reflect on what she might do to initiate 2 + 2 observations at Dewey High. School wouldn't begin for a few weeks, but Joy wanted to plan a first step while she had the time to think about it. The 2 + 2 idea seemed so full of common sense. Besides, Joy found herself intrigued with the idea of visiting other classrooms. She hadn't seen anyone teach since her student teaching days, which were now all but forgotten. *The main thing,* she thought, *is to get started.* 2 + 2 sounded like something that could be tried informally. But how should she begin?

Start small, she thought to herself. Clearly there would need to be a group of teachers to visit one another, and, of course, the teachers Joy knew best were English teachers. The school was so large that she didn't know many teachers outside the floor where her classroom was situated. She had a couple of contacts among teachers with the same lunch schedule and knew a couple of others on the social committee.

Maybe, she theorized, *the 2 + 2 observations could begin to change that. With time, of course, but let's be practical. It's the middle of summer vacation. Who can I call in the department? Definitely Paige,* Joy decided. Paige was a fellow English teacher and one of her best friends. *Terry would probably be open to the idea also.* Terry was the well-regarded English depart-

> Find the teachers who are willing to try 2 + 2.

ment chairperson, and Joy had always wished she could see what went on inside her classroom. But Paige and Terry, it turned out, were vacationing out of town.

She wondered about Andy. He seemed like a conscientious teacher and was always friendly and pleasant. She was a little nervous. Although she respected Andy and wished she knew him better, she wasn't sure how he'd react to the 2 + 2 proposal. But 2 + 2 wasn't just for people she knew well.

Andy had just returned from a trip to Europe and was both relaxed and invigorated when Joy called. She explained the 2 + 2 program and asked him to be part of a small group engaged in 2 + 2 observations. "It will begin with just a few department colleagues," she said, "and perhaps grow to include others throughout the school." Andy was both surprised and pleased that Joy would call him with such an innovative proposal. He couldn't help being swayed by her enthusiasm. On top of that, he was rather excited at the prospect of seeing his colleagues at work. True, the thought of others observing him was a little unnerving, but it seemed a fair trade-off. He could hardly pass up the opportunity to gain some insights into his own teaching, especially after his frustrating experience with the last performance appraisal.

When Joy finally connected with Paige and Terry in the following weeks, she encountered more positive reactions. Paige was definitely interested. Terry was enthused despite her overloaded schedule. She had long thought that there was too little sharing of teaching expertise in the school.

In Joy's entire career, no one had ever mentioned visiting other teachers' classrooms, and yet the first three teachers she called on embraced the idea wholeheartedly. They even seemed to be excited about receiving feedback on their own teaching. Their responses reinforced Joy's conviction that the 2 + 2 concept could be a success at Dewey High.

Joy suggested, and they all agreed, that they meet during the teacher workweek before school opened in August to finalize their plans. Joy also agreed with Terry's suggestion to meet with the principal, so Sissy wouldn't be out of the loop. The 2 + 2 experiment was entirely informal, and the school was so large Sissy might never even know about their 2 + 2 pilot, but it just seemed reasonable to get her go-ahead. "I wonder what Sissy will think of the program," Joy said aloud as she called the school to make an appointment to see Sissy the following week.

Teachers Talk About 2 + 2

- "The 2 + 2 concept decreases my isolation and makes me feel more a part of a team effort. It's an excellent tool for teacher growth."
- "2 + 2 has got to be the very best way for teachers to help other teachers improve."
- "The 2 + 2 program has enabled me as a seasoned teacher to gain meaningful insights and new ideas as I visit my peers."
- "I feel that the compliments listed gave me a lot of positive reinforcement. They also gave me encouragement to try additional innovative and creative activities to help my students grasp the concepts . . .
- "This process has led me to a better understanding of the working of our faculty as a whole."
- "I would like to try more interdisciplinary projects with other teachers . . . 2 + 2 has helped me to understand better how we can interrelate some of the disciplines."
- "Many times, we have been doing something a certain way for so long, it is not until someone else points it out that we can begin to correct it."
- "This program gives teachers a choice that was not available before. Choice promotes empowerment, creativity, and good morale . . . the 2 + 2 program opens lines of communication among teachers, which could possibly lead to cooperative teaching endeavors."
- "It is an opportunity for teachers to help teachers by sharing their expertise."
- "I have had the opportunity to share teaching ideas and become acquainted with other disciplines . . .
- "I like to think of 2 + 2 as a means for teachers to help teachers. If done thoughtfully and reflectively, it accomplishes this!"
- "I plan to get out of my little box more often to visit other classes. The 2 + 2 process has allowed me to share as well as obtain so many new ideas and teaching strategies."

2 + 2 Classroom Observation Form

Teacher: _____　　School: _____

Observer: _____　　Date: _____

Grade:_____　　Subject: _____

Size of Class/Arrangement: _____

1. Compliments:

   1.

   2.

2. Suggestions:

   1.

   2.

Reflections:

4

The Feedback Dilemma

The quick fix is an attempt to solve a complex problem by addressing the symptoms of the problem rather than the fundamental root causes. A quick fix doesn't solve the problem. Moreover, the use of quick fixes can make the fundamental problem more difficult to identify and a fundamental solution more difficult to implement. In schools, inadequate professional development is a complex problem. A typical quick fix is the traditional teacher inservice day that gives the appearance of professional development support. The quick fix helps obscure the fundamental problem that professional development opportunities for teachers are not a serious priority for many school systems. Teacher accountability is also a complex problem. An accountability quick fix is the traditional performance appraisal. The traditional appraisal process, involving a few visits from an administrator, gives only the appearance of accountability. The fundamental problem of a teaching environment lacking in feedback, follow-up, encouragement, improvement, and accountability is thereby masked and compounded.

An Administrator's View: Staff Development Revisited

Sissy sat in her office deep in thought during a rare moment of quiet near the end of the summer. While paperwork and district duties continued to occupy much of her time, summers were also a time of reflection. Summer school sessions were over. The building, except for the bare-bones minimum secretarial staff, was now empty. Workers and technicians finished building renovations and the installation of new technology only the day before. Later that day, Joy would be coming in to see her, but for now Sissy felt relaxed and refreshed.

Still, she couldn't help but think how soon the relative calm would give way to a typical school day—conferences with parents, district meetings, faculty meetings, meetings with individual teachers and union representatives, e-mails needing responses, documents to prepare, reports to write, situations to anticipate and react to . . .

Administrative duties are one thing I can really count on in this job, Sissy concluded. *But what about my role as the instructional leader of the school? I'm not getting it all done,* she thought with some frustration. *How can I be a better instructional leader when I'm swamped with managerial duties and daily crises? To think that when I took this job I imagined setting just the opposite priorities! At this point, I can only pay attention to teaching and instruction in dribs and drabs. I feel like I'm continually being sidetracked. Yet I'd like to see myself as an instructional leader.*

True, meetings with parents and community members are enjoyable, she thought, *and for the most part, I even look forward to faculty meetings. Still, I wish I knew how to do more than just keep everyone up-to-date on the latest district initiatives.* Sissy knew she had a staff development role to play and a responsibility to provide direction and guidance for teachers. She was also sure of the direction she wanted the school to move in. She was aware of the research on a more interdisciplinary approach to teaching, on alternative assessment methods, on awareness of different learning styles, and on the importance of a large repertoire of teaching strategies. The learning process should relate to a child's world of experience; standards, curriculum, and assessment should be aligned; and teachers should care about all of their students and show it. Sissy kept up with her professional journals. New research and ideas were continually debated. But it wasn't enough for her to *know*—she also had to lead. How could she promote an awareness of the need for the whole school to change? All she had accomplished by mandating interdisciplinary units, she feared, was to create more resistance. But if teachers weren't going to move ahead on their own, what could she do but force the issue? Maybe the dead wood would transfer or resign.

She thought back on a meeting earlier that summer with the assistant superintendent for curriculum. He had briefed the district's principals on the latest state education initiatives. "I don't need to tell any of you that times have changed," he had said. "That much is obvious. Accountability is what we're about. We need to continue to show progress on standardized tests for all students. Teachers, principals, schools, and districts are all held accountable by the state for standardized test results. There's even talk of a public report card that will list test results by school and possibly by classroom. A school that doesn't meet minimum standards after three years of testing could possibly have its staff dismissed. But standardized test scores are only part of our focus. Most important is the need to focus on improving student outcomes, as measured in many different ways, through better planning and delivery of instruction and assessment.

"I know we have some of the best teachers anywhere right here in this district. But we still have a long way to go in terms of student achievement, in closing the achievement gap, and we still have far too many dropouts. So it's really up to each of you to ensure that quality teaching is going on in your schools. We can't afford for anyone to be satisfied with the status quo.

"I'd like to be able to tell you that additional funding for staff development or for special programs will be available next year. Unfortunately, that won't happen. The money has already been committed for computers and other areas of need. The good news is that the technology initiative will progress on schedule, with work on the five remaining schools in the district currently without a fiber optics network to be completed over the summer."

He had ended the meeting with a reminder that new curriculum guides reflecting better alignment of state standards of learning and standardized assessments would be available for the elementary grades by the fall start of school. Middle and high school guides would take another year to complete.

No surprises there, Sissy remembered. *But how would even the new computers and other equipment really begin to benefit students until teachers had adequate training to incorporate them into their teaching? Once again, professional support and development are being shortchanged. And I'm going to be held accountable for how well the teachers and the kids perform.* Sissy was not comforted by the thought.

> In today's schools, professional support and development are often shortchanged.

Sissy was well aware of her limited powers to make changes where they really mattered—behind classroom doors. She had also become increasingly aware that the enormous independence enjoyed by teachers could be a great weakness as well as a formidable strength. Teachers' autonomy allowed them to adapt to the needs of each classroom situation. The flexibility for creative and innovative approaches and the freedom to adopt new ideas and to experiment required independent judgment, of course. But there were no consequences for closing the door and teaching the same way for twenty-five years—and often no incentives to do otherwise.

Sissy believed that if teachers would reflect on their practice and experiment with new ideas, improvement would be inevitable. Could increases in student performance be far behind? Why didn't this happen more often? Perhaps teachers had the desire to improve but didn't know how to go about it. She also knew a few teachers who were convinced they didn't need to change anything—that it was the students who needed to change. Regardless of the specific elements on her agenda, she knew that time and staff development would be required for teaching behaviors to change. Yet how could that happen without help?

In all fairness, Sissy thought, *teachers are being asked to do more and more, in the same amount of time and with a more challenging student body.* She recalled how she had felt as a teacher. There had never been enough time to attend to all the needs of each child. New programs, or for that matter any changes, required extra effort. Even then, feedback on her performance and support for making changes were virtually nonexistent. *Not so different from my job as an administrator,* she thought a little ruefully.

What did staff development look like at Dewey High? Staff development days, informally known as inservice days, were scheduled for one afternoon a month. That limited time was devoted to professional development. But despite Sissy's attempts to plan sessions relevant to teaching and best curricular practices, inservice days were often taken up with guests from the district who explained new policies. Staff development had too often become a euphemism for housekeeping chores or news updates, where the latest district news or information was passed on to the front line. Instead of a coordinated program of professional development, a potpourri of topics received a light dusting of attention. Sometimes curriculum people from downtown used these days to meet with individual academic departments. Such meetings seemed to add to the fragmentation of departments that was already a hindrance to good communication within the school. There was no time for follow-up, much less ongoing staff development. She admitted she couldn't see much evidence that improvements were happening. Even when a workshop was planned around an instructional issue, the one- or two-shot inoculation approach wasn't working. *Or was it?* she thought wryly. *The vaccination approach almost guaranteed that teachers wouldn't get it.*

What exactly is staff development? she reflected. Sissy thought back to a conversation she'd had with the deputy superintendent just last week. He made a habit of dropping in on schools just to touch base and consult with principals. Bill had said, "I really think that, ideally, staff development is something continuous—an ongoing process. Actually, the word *development* implies a progression, or growth, toward a more advanced state, doesn't it? The question is, where is the time and money going to come from to encourage and support that progression? Sorry to say, I can't offer you much support in terms of extra time or funding. As a former principal, though, I know that anything new you want to introduce, like interdisciplinary teaming, is going to need a lot of faculty commitment. It's also going to require some opportunities for training and follow-up. What we really need is to get people to talk to each other about educational issues. You've got to build the desire in your faculty to work and collaborate together. Some positive faculty leadership won't solve everything, but it would sure help."

> Effective staff development must lead to a desire to collaborate and work together.

Sissy wondered whether it was possible to look beyond the once-a-month-for-two-hours approach to staff development. How could she design a development process that would support continuous improvement for her teachers? A process to help teachers explore and grow by degrees?

An Administrator's View: Performance Appraisal Revisited

What about performance appraisals? she thought. *Isn't that a form of staff development?* She remembered she had already struggled with those questions during last spring's appraisal write-ups.

Sissy had asked Bill about that, too. "Well," he had replied with a smile, "theoretically I suppose you could make that argument because professional growth is what the appraisal developers like to say is the purpose of the exercise. In reality, I've always found performance appraisal useful when a teacher was marginal or incompetent. Otherwise, I've never found it to be a very efficient or effective professional development tool."

As she went over the conversation in her head, she realized something for the first time. *The truth is that I have to agree with Bill. Perhaps the appraisal process not only seems like a waste of time but is in fact an exercise in futility.*

Premise of Professional Development

- Most teachers are competent and able.
- Most teachers want to grow and improve their professional practice.
- The purpose of both performance appraisal and inservice training for competent teachers is improvement of instruction.

Problems With Traditional Professional Development

- Most teachers have learned through experience that one-shot workshops can provide good ideas, but they have also learned the following drawbacks:
    1. Time in the regular school day to try ideas out in a systematic way is inadequate.
    2. Teacher isolation makes implementation of ideas difficult to impossible since no feedback is available for teachers on how they're doing.
- A few individual teachers may attempt to improve their own practice through workshops or seminars, but transfer is iffy, and it's not enough to transform a school.
- Most teachers are not afforded the opportunity to view the teaching performance of others. Uncertainty about the state of the profession and one's own place in the profession is a consequence of this practice.
- Performance appraisal is of limited usefulness for the following reasons:
    1. Feedback is infrequent, often lacking specificity and follow-up.
    2. Feedback is from one source only.
    3. Anxiety and negativity often accompany the process.
    4. Performance appraisal instruments are subjective yet purport to be objective.
    5. Performance appraisal instruments often work best to document seriously deficient teaching performance instead of promoting the improvement of competent performance.

Effective Professional Development

- Three keys to successful professional development are as follows:
    1. Frequent, specific feedback on teaching performance, including recognition of positive elements and suggestions for improvement, from a variety of sources
    2. Opportunities to observe other professionals' teaching performance and to offer feedback
    3. The reduction of teacher isolation and the development of collaborative relationships fostered through giving and receiving feedback

For better or worse, the appraisal cycle at Dewey High was three years. Sissy's staff was so large, though, that evaluating even one third of the faculty each year was a major task. She had two assistant principals to help her, but she liked to maintain close contact with the appraisal process because it was one of her few chances to influence teacher improvement. Besides, performance appraisal helped define her role as principal. But because observations were few and follow-up was next to impossible, she couldn't know whether appraisals had any direct relationship with professional development.

What did teachers think of the whole process? she wondered. *Was it of any use to them?*

A thought suddenly came to her. "I've all but forgotten about the teacher feedback from last year!" she exclaimed.

She went to the file cabinet and rummaged through the old appraisal folders. She had solicited teacher feedback about the per-formance appraisal system but hadn't gotten around to reviewing it. Sissy had an idea that teachers were as unhappy with the appraisal system as she was. This concerned her because she knew that nega-tive attitudes could undermine whatever benefit teachers might potentially receive from the appraisal process.

She retrieved the files, scanned the anonymous responses, and noted few positive comments. Someone wrote that "the appraisal system is fine," and someone else thought "the appraisal system gives one a very objective and realistic outcome of a person's total effectiveness in a classroom." However, most of the comments were negative.

One teacher wrote that the current system "requires the evaluator to make judgments on things where there's no practical way to judge unless that person were to sit in my classroom and observe over a long period of time—which doesn't happen."

Others found that it "rated teachers but didn't help improve performance," and they called the most recent revisions "complicated and ineffective."

One of Sissy's apparently best teachers wrote, "I usually receive the highest rating, but I'm not sure it's a fair appraisal because I never get any constructive feedback—and I just don't believe that anyone's perfect."

Sissy continued leafing through the file. Even the teachers who responded positively seemed to qualify their answers:

- "I've had success with this system and have received good ratings. But oftentimes I thought that the administrators were making things up since I couldn't recall some of what they brought up in the conferences."

- "Teachers generally are given all of the 'glows' and none of the 'grows' that they need to have."
- "It's okay. I just don't think it's an effective tool."

Then there were the entirely negative comments:

- "Very stressful."
- "The performance appraisal system is frequently misused."
- "The person doing the evaluation always tries to find something wrong/nitpicky."
- "Too subjective."
- "Three observations are not enough to key on different competencies."
- "I don't care for it. An assistant principal—a former social studies teacher—wouldn't know about health and PE or understand the learning taking place when it looks like chaos."
- "As far as trying to help people improve performance, I don't think it does a good job."
- "I don't think that it's helpful. It is basically a checklist and there is no feedback."

> Our current system of performance appraisal doesn't please anyone and has little impact on practice.

Sissy was just a little surprised at the bluntness of some of the comments. Of course, performance appraisal wasn't necessarily intended to be fun or pleasant. But wait! Hadn't she always considered the performance appraisal to be an opportunity to help teachers improve? Hadn't she always thought of the performance appraisal as a positive exercise? Why should there be anything unpleasant about an appraisal, as long as it was framed in the context of professional development? But teachers were certainly skeptical about getting anything helpful out of it. And some seemed pretty defensive, too.

Thinking about the last round of performance appraisals, she realized she hadn't exactly looked forward to them either. *So why am I so surprised?* she thought. *Probably because I'm trying to make performance appraisal fit a staff development model, while in actual practice the performance appraisal system seems designed to catch flaws rather than build on strengths or offer constructive feedback. Come to think of it, I even end up feeling defensive. I have to judge a teacher's performance and justify a rating on the basis of a few isolated observations. This snapshot-in-time approach is enough to see that a teacher is not incompetent but not enough to provide any real support.*

Sissy put the files away and wandered over to the window, deep in thought. *What is the real point of appraisal? I know that more than 90% of my teaching staff is competent. Some are truly exceptional. Each, of course, has strengths and weaknesses. If performance appraisal were truly useful, it would facilitate improvement of each teacher's performance. Apparently though, a much different perception exists among the teachers about the usefulness of performance appraisal. The teachers' comments indicate that while they would welcome more feedback and help in improving performance, the traditional appraisal instrument just isn't the right vehicle.*

How to approach the issues of performance appraisal, staff development, and instructional feedback was going to require more thinking. Sissy began to worry anew about pressures from the district to improve student outcomes. She didn't have a chance to worry for long, however, for at that moment Joy arrived.

5

The 2 + 2 Pilot

An elephant was brought into a dark room at night for an exhibition. The people streamed by in throngs. Since it was dark, the visitors couldn't see the elephant, so they tried to get an idea of his body by touching him. Because he was large, each visitor could only grab a part of the animal and describe it according to what he had felt. One of the visitors, who had gotten hold of a leg, explained that the elephant was like a mighty pillar; a second one, who touched a tusk, described the elephant as a pointy object; a third, who grabbed the creature's ear, claimed he was not different from a fan; the fourth, who ran his hand over the elephant's back, stated that the elephant was as flat as a couch.

—Traditional Indian fable

Are teachers in the dark about how their teaching, their colleagues' teaching, and the teaching profession looks?

Joy's Visit

Sissy was curious about what Joy had on her mind. What was 2 + 2? As they exchanged greetings, Sissy motioned for Joy to join her at the conference table.

"First of all," Joy began, "thank you for agreeing to meet during the summer. I know how busy you are. I didn't want to go any further, though, without your input."

"It's no problem at all, Joy," said Sissy with a smile. "In fact, today is especially quiet. It's good to see a familiar face around the building. What's on your mind?"

"I was at one of Dr. James's workshops a few weeks ago," Joy related. "He talked about teacher isolation, stress, uncertainty, and the lack of feedback teachers get about their own teaching performance. Then he introduced this 2 + 2 program." Joy handed Sissy a copy of the material that she'd received at Dr. James's presentation. "You can have a look at that when you have time, but I can explain what 2 + 2 is all about. 2 + 2 means two compliments and two suggestions. It's what teachers write as they're observing one another teach."

Joy explained the basic premise of the 2 + 2 program—feedback and encouragement. "Teachers are pretty isolated," she continued. "2 + 2 could help teachers improve by providing a way for us to receive feedback from our colleagues. The point is to gain the perspective of a number of different teachers. And," she emphasized, "it would be wonderful to observe what other teachers are doing in their classrooms. Andy, Paige, Terry, and I have discussed starting a 2 + 2 group this fall. We hope others will want to participate as time goes on. But before getting started, we wanted to ask what you think about it."

> The case for peer observation— a relatively small investment with potentially large returns.

Sissy nodded her head in encouragement, as she tried to piece the 2 + 2 idea together. "Well, I can't see anything wrong with peer observation," she said. "In fact, the idea of peer observation has been around for a long time, though it's not practiced very often. I'd like to congratulate you all on your initiative. But what exactly does the program entail? Is there conferencing? Any requirements beyond writing two compliments and two suggestions?"

Joy briefly reviewed the anatomy of a 2 + 2 visit, showed Sissy a copy of a 2 + 2 observation form, and mentioned that the observation itself did not need to be lengthy. "I think that's how we're going to manage frequent observations," she added, "because the idea is for teachers to observe one another, and to be observed, many times over a semester. So you see, the program is really simple and streamlined."

Sissy wondered silently whether its simplicity might also be its weakness. She knew from the professional literature that peer observation could be worthwhile, but she still questioned whether teachers could really critique their friends and colleagues. In addition, the 2 + 2 form was rather abbreviated, indeed.

Although Sissy wasn't completely convinced that 2 + 2 would be a worthwhile investment of time and energy, she did know that teachers apparently weren't satisfied with the quality of performance appraisal feedback they were currently receiving. Anyway, what harm could come of teachers observing each other?

"I have an idea," Sissy suggested. "You go ahead with the 2 + 2 program with anyone who'd like to participate. It'll be a pilot program. At the end of the semester, report back to me what you and the others think of it. Perhaps you can also let me have a look at some of the 2 + 2 compliments and suggestions people are sharing with each other."

Joy was pleased at Sissy's response, but her last request made Joy nervous. "I'm not sure teachers would want to share their comments. I mean, someone might have written something that wasn't quite accurate . . ."

"If it makes you more comfortable, I suppose you could remove the names from the feedback forms," Sissy agreed, "although it could well be that someone would want to share particularly favorable comments. But for now, it doesn't really matter. I'd just like to see the kind of feedback teachers are giving and getting from the program."

Joy agreed and thanked Sissy for her support. "I'll get back to you with some information on 2 + 2 later in the semester," she promised.

2 + 2: The Initial Experiment

During the teacher workweek before school opened in August, Joy and her group solidified their 2 + 2 plans. Joy shared the basic 2 + 2 protocol handout and the 2 + 2 Classroom Observation Form she'd gotten at Dr. James's workshop and mentioned that he would be available to answer any questions that might come up. They all agreed that frequent visits were a key element of the program and planned to visit one classroom each week. Everyone was comfortable with the idea that no prior notice was necessary. After all, they wanted to stick to their normal routine without having 2 + 2 become a disruption. Nonetheless, they decided that each teacher could always ask an observer to come again at a different time. For example, there could be a problem that needed to be addressed only within the classroom, or perhaps the teacher was about to administer a test.

The school year opened with its usual flurry of meetings, changed schedules, and general chaos. It was mid-September before routines began to normalize, and Joy realized that 2 + 2 had dropped out of sight. She resolved then and there to use half her daily planning period to visit Paige. She felt a little awkward just walking into Paige's classroom, but there was no time to ask permission. Anyway, they'd all agreed to show up whenever time permitted. Joy grabbed one of the 2 + 2 forms and was delighted when Paige waved her in. Joy recognized several students in the room. How different it was to see them in another classroom! Paige immediately had the class on task, and students didn't seem to object to another teacher in the room. Joy admired the easy rapport Paige established with the class. Other compliments came to mind easily.

Suggestions were another matter. During the discussion of a short story, the class seemed engaged and interested. What could she possibly say? Then, Joy remembered a successful lesson she had taught involving a similar piece of literature. She had divided the class into teams and had given each team a different essay question to discuss. The teams then had to present their arguments and subsequently defend their conclusions in a Q & A session. That might be a possible alternative Paige could consider for a future lesson. At a loss for a second suggestion, she noticed that several students near the back were uninvolved and probably having difficulty hearing what was going on. She decided to suggest an alternative seating arrangement.

Twenty minutes later, Joy was back in her own classroom. She wasn't sure what Paige would think of what she'd written, but the visit had stimulated her thinking. How refreshing to visit another classroom and observe someone else teach! Hopefully someone would visit her soon.

> Trying something new always involves risk.

Joy did not have to wait long. The next day, Terry dropped into Joy's classroom. Students were still filing into the second-period class, and Joy had a moment to help Terry find an empty chair before class began. She was reassured to find that it was not threatening to have a colleague in the room. In fact, it helped her focus on what she was doing. When Terry left twenty minutes later, Joy found herself eager for the period to end so she could read the 2 + 2 feedback. She smiled to herself as she read Terry's compliments. She was pleased that Terry had noticed how she tried to connect the issues in the text with the students' life experiences. As for the suggestions, she was particularly attentive to Terry's comment that the students should be encouraged to develop related topics for further research by facilitating a brainstorming session. Joy realized that she had gotten out of the habit of using student input as much as she had in the past. She hadn't even thought about it much lately. Simply assigning work had slowly become the norm. Maybe it was time to reconsider her approach. She smiled. *How long would it have taken me to figure this out on my own?* she wondered.

And so it continued for several weeks. Andy was delighted to have his colleagues validate his careful preparation and command of the material. Interestingly, several suggestions focused on his pre-disposition to lecture, rather than to teach interactively. He recalled how Sissy had made similar comments during his performance appraisal last year. Somehow his colleagues' feedback seemed less threatening. Perhaps it was because a performance rating wasn't rid-ing on each visit. Or maybe he felt his colleagues had a better handle on actual classroom practice. Andy found, at any rate, that his col-leagues could give him concrete suggestions for alternative teaching strategies. And, increasingly, he looked for ways on his own to gen-erate more class participation. Since he could expect a 2 + 2 visit at any time, he hoped to receive feedback that would reflect the changes he'd made.

Perhaps even more stimulating were his visits to the other classrooms. As he discovered new ideas, his confidence in his own teaching improved. Other teachers, it seemed, had their own classroom management challenges. At the same time, he had observed that certain students did not always behave the same way in other classes as they did in his classroom. This gave him a different perspective on how best to reach those students.

Gradually, word got around that some of the English teachers were observing and cri-tiquing each other. First a math teacher and then a social studies teacher asked Joy if she would observe them. Sure, said Joy, if they would return the favor. Andy, Paige, and Terry received similar requests. By the end of November, about a dozen teachers had visited each other at least once and completed a 2 + 2 observation form.

> Early success that spreads through word of mouth can inspire others to try something new.

While the 2 + 2 idea began to circulate among the staff, Joy sud-denly realized that a few weeks had gone by since she had observed anyone. Her observations and feedback had certainly been worth-while, but so many other things needed her attention. She wondered how many of her colleagues were having the same problem. A few teachers had commented positively about 2 + 2, but she still felt pretty much in the dark about how it was going. Joy thought of Sissy's request for information on the pilot 2 + 2 and decided it might be use-ful to have a meeting of 2 + 2 participants to see what the other teachers were thinking.

Initial Feedback on the 2 + 2 Pilot

A week later, twelve teachers gathered to review the 2 + 2 program. Joy expected to hear mostly positive reports, but even she was unprepared for the high level of enthusiasm. "After twenty-five years of teaching," exclaimed one teacher, "I finally made it out of my department and onto another floor. I've visited a technology class, a math class, and a science class, and I've seen ideas that will make me a better teacher." Joy tried several times to get an opposing viewpoint, but the teachers had nothing negative to report about the value of the 2 + 2 program or the validity of its rationale.

> The excitement of overcoming years of isolation can energize teachers.

Surprisingly, many teachers' comments made a direct comparison between the traditional performance appraisal observation and 2 + 2 observations. One teacher said the following—to general agreement— "I think the typical appraisal method is ineffective and not very helpful. But I think 2 + 2 is effective and helpful because my peers are making the observations. When they come in and suggest that I work on my questioning techniques, they're not saying that they do it better. They're just saying that it's something to work on. I agree with that, and it's appreciated. I wish I'd had this as a new teacher."

Someone else added, "When I think of the difference between how I teach today and how I taught twenty years ago, I realize that the things I've learned to do well, I did not learn from an administrator or a department head. If we'd been doing 2 + 2 then, there's no telling what I could have gotten from being the observer. In my cluster, which is predominantly math and science, it's been really helpful to see how they do things differently in social studies."

Other teachers also remarked on the contrast between peer and administrator visits. Paige commented, "If another teacher comes in, the students are much less likely to pay attention to the person. If a principal comes in, the students are likely to act differently and throw you off."

Another put it this way: "To have peers come in is not as intimidating. I feel I can continue working, not making a lot of changes in what I'm doing for the benefit of the observer. I can be the real me and just work with what's going on in my real teaching."

> The 2 + 2 process can sell itself.

Initial enthusiasm for the program was clearly unanimous. As the praise ran its course, though, it became apparent that there were still several sticking points. Some were just implementation questions, such as the misconception that a visit had to occur at the beginning of the class. "In fact," Joy explained, "an observation can begin at any point during the class period. That gives everyone maximum flexibility. It also allows the observer to see more than just the class warm-up every time."

Other issues were more substantive. Joy knew that most of the teachers hadn't done more than a few 2 + 2 observations, and she wasn't surprised to learn that many thought time was an issue. "I'm willing to use my planning period if I have to," said one teacher, "but there is so little time as it is for preparation. I find I really have to make 2 + 2 a priority to get out of my room. But then I'm always glad when I do." So many teachers agreed that time was an obstacle to 2 + 2 observations that Joy began wondering if anything could be done to alleviate the time pressure.

Another difficulty was related to giving and receiving suggestions. Although suggestions were generally received in a spirit of trust and appreciation, Joy noted two situations where suggestions were causing some irritation: when a suggestion was made to remedy a situation beyond the teacher's control and when someone suggested a strategy that the teacher actually used before the visitor came in or after the visitor left the classroom.

For example, one teacher said, "Each day I need to get the exact number of books at the beginning of class from another social studies teacher since we share the set. If a student comes in late, I won't have a book for that student. When another teacher makes a comment about the fact that there aren't enough books, I feel as though I've been unfairly criticized and that I need to explain myself."

Another teacher commented, "When I read the 2 + 2 forms and read what was positive, I can make up my own mind whether I agree or not. And I take a look at the suggestions and try to put myself in the observer's place to see what they were thinking. If it looks like a misunderstanding, I just ignore it. Or sometimes it's good to contact them and discuss the issue, even just for the sake of sharing information."

"Maybe that's good," said Andy. "I mean, it's good that more discussion is taking place. Everyone who's observed me, we've just talked, you know, in passing. I think it's just natural. After I observed one person in particular, we talked and discussed so many different ideas."

In general, the teachers agreed that more discussion was taking place. One teacher remarked, "I think the informal

> Informal feedback and improved collegiality are some of the most important benefits of exchanging classroom visits.

feedback that you exchange with each other is part of the value of 2 + 2, whether it happens a few days later or a week later."

Most felt that making suggestions presented its own challenges. Some even argued there wasn't always a need to write suggestions when none came to mind during an excellent lesson. They objected to writing something down just because it was required, and a number of them admitted leaving the suggestions section blank. Still others formulated suggestions as "continue with" statements, such as "continue with your Socratic method" or whatever the positive teaching strategy was. As the discussion continued, it was evident that many teachers simply weren't sure how to improve their skills at making meaningful suggestions.

"You know, for all of us, visiting other teachers and offering feedback is a new experience," Joy observed. "Is there some way we could get some training on how to make suggestions? Do you think that would be useful? None of us has actually been taught how to observe teaching performance."

"I don't think we really need formal training," said one business teacher. "I do think that meetings such as this one are helpful, though. Maybe we could see what kinds of suggestions everyone else is making and get an idea of what's expected. I also think sharing our 2 + 2 experiences is motivating. It makes me want to do more observations."

Others agreed that more informal meetings to touch base would be welcome. Privately, Joy was concerned that some of her colleagues didn't understand the importance of making suggestions. *But,* she thought, *maybe it's a matter of practice. At least they seem open to learning better feedback skills.*

Discussion returned several times to the issue of who was participating in 2 + 2. If more teachers participated, a music teacher commented, not only would observations be easier to schedule but also a wider variety of feedback would be possible. Teachers also requested more clearly defined guidelines for participation. Some believed the informality of the pilot made it harder to make 2 + 2 observations a priority.

Finally, was there any way a formal 2 + 2 program could be made part of the appraisal process? After all, if 2 + 2 were firmly established, teachers would receive many more observations from a variety of professionals throughout the year than the formal appraisal process afforded them. Surely that would provide a more accurate picture of their performance. This was something Joy hadn't considered. She wondered what Sissy would think of that.

Joy was more than satisfied with the range and depth of the feedback. The whole meeting itself—with its give and take—had been a new experience. Her initial belief that 2 + 2 was an excellent program had certainly been confirmed. Now she had the feeling that they hadn't really even begun to explore its potential. She agreed that they needed more information about how to expand the program and possibly add a performance appraisal component. Before approaching Sissy, however, she wanted to have a better idea about how to proceed with 2 + 2 from its originator. After all, this had been just an informal experiment so far. *This would be a good time to visit Dr. James,* she thought. She decided to do exactly that.

6

2 + 2 Takes Shape

Implementation of 2 + 2 may be an iterative process. Gradually, more details are addressed, details that have emerged through the pilot program experiences. In the process, focus on the program's purpose and spirit grows stronger.

In early December, Joy headed for Dr. James's office at the university. Dr. James was pleased to see her again. "I remember you well, Joy," he said. "It's good to see you. How's everything going? Still stirring things up? You had quite a reputation as a firebrand when you were here, you know."

"Thank you, Dr. James," replied Joy, pleased at the warm welcome. "Things are going very well. You've always been a role model for me with your ideas about learning and teaching. Actually, you still are. I heard your presentation last summer about the 2 + 2 program, and a small group of us began observing one another this fall. We're enjoying the observations, but I could use some advice."

"That's what I'm here for," replied Dr. James.

Joy explained how she had informally initiated 2 + 2 with a few colleagues and how it had begun to expand well beyond the original group. She related what her fellow teachers had to say about 2 + 2, as well as the plan to develop a formal, schoolwide 2 + 2 program. Would it be possible to use 2 + 2 as part of an appraisal system? She could see the effect 2 + 2 was already having as teachers were beginning to talk about actual classroom observations—across disciplines, amazingly.

Surely Sissy, who had mandated interdisciplinary units, would be pleased at this development.

Dr. James listened with interest to her report. "I give you a lot of credit for trying to implement the 2 + 2 program on your own, and it sounds like it's going very well. You've seen from the feedback you've received just how valuable it can be, though I'm not at all surprised by the positive responses from your teachers. Teachers crave feedback and encouragement. They are naturally diplomatic givers of feedback, too. If anything, I would bet that many are too diplomatic to key in on some of the larger problems. That will come as they build

> The 2 + 2 system of feedback can be used for both formal and informal feedback and performance appraisal.

trust among themselves and gain experience in the process. Formalizing the 2 + 2 program seems a logical next step in making this a schoolwide initiative. Leadership from your administration could be an important key to its success."

Joy agreed. "Sissy knows about the pilot, of course, and wants me to report what teachers think of it at the end of the semester. She seemed to be interested in the program when I explained it. I agree that to really get serious about 2 + 2 we'll need more than her permission. We'll need her commitment to the whole idea. I think it would help if I had a plan to present to her for a schoolwide implementation when I see her. That should be by next week. If we wait much longer, there won't be enough lead time to get organized."

Dr. James thought for a moment. "Sissy seems to be a very capable administrator. I know her from a course she took several years ago. Once she hears about your conversations with teachers about 2 + 2, I hope she will be receptive to the idea of a schoolwide observation program. As you say, her support is essential. In fact, her active commitment to the 2 + 2 program would help many teachers realize that their participation in 2 + 2 isn't going to put them in jeopardy with the administration. Her support would also communicate the importance she attaches to the program, substantially raising its profile around the school. The more she knows about the 2 + 2 process, the more likely she'll be to provide the leadership. By the way, she and the principals + assistant principals should become active participants. 2 + 2 is not just a peer observation program, after all."

"I'd completely forgotten about that," exclaimed Joy.

"For that matter," Dr. James continued, "your students could be involved in 2 + 2 feedback, too."

> Student 2 + 2s can provide important perspectives for teachers.

Student 2 + 2s! This was new to Joy. Had she missed that last summer? She couldn't quite suppress a show of skepticism.

Dr. James laughed. "You might get some strange responses from your students, but you might be surprised by their insight if you let them know you take their feedback seriously. Remember, you aren't obligated to act on any of the feedback, but at least you'll know where they're coming from. Wouldn't any teacher want to know that?"

Joy considered this for a moment. "I can't imagine any teacher not wanting to know that. But I can imagine teachers being afraid of the feedback they might receive."

"Teachers can direct their request for feedback toward a particular lesson or project, rather than asking for a critique of their teaching practice," Dr. James offered in response. "Ask students what was interesting about a new lesson and what might have made it better. You might suggest it to your colleagues sometime. I'll wager one of them will try it out.

"So you see, both administrative and student feedback are elements to include in your second round of 2 + 2. Another component of a more structured 2 + 2 program is the reflection process. Naturally, one hopes that teachers will reflect on

> The reflection process is an important part of 2 + 2 and professional growth.

their feedback. It's the reflection on the experience that will influence growth and change. For that reason, I would suggest that teachers write a short reflection report at the close of each semester. In my experience, most teachers have found it to be a useful exercise."

Dr. James gave Joy a form with sample reflection questions. "Feel free to alter the form if you wish," he said. "Your teachers may want to consider other questions for reflection." Joy looked over the form, which appeared quite straightforward and simple. "Thank you," she said. "This is going to be very useful."

"When completed," Dr. James continued, "the reflection report may become part of a teacher's portfolio or, ideally, their performance appraisal. In fact, in some schools, 2 + 2 has become the performance appraisal and has replaced the traditional model. This comes back to your question about using 2 + 2 as part of a performance appraisal system at your school. I'm not sure whether Sissy would be willing to take the risk of using 2 + 2 in lieu of the district's performance appraisal system. For that matter, it's not likely that she could, unless she was willing to take it up with the school district. Making it an optional component of the appraisal process is always a possibility, however. Teachers could discuss their reflective self-evaluation as part of the appraisal conference. Sissy could give credit for participation in 2 + 2 by documenting it under one of the traditional performance appraisal domains as well. Even if 2 + 2 coexisted at first with the traditional appraisal model, making these connections with formal performance

2 + 2 Reflection Report

Name: _____   School: _____

Grade Level/
Subject Area: _____   Semester: _____

1. List the ten most useful/significant compliments received.

2. List the ten most useful/significant suggestions received.

3. Analysis: Explain which of the above compliments and suggestions were especially useful and how they have led to reinforcement or improvement of your classroom teaching routines. List any future agenda items that have emerged as a result of the 2 + 2 process.

4. List the five most helpful ideas gleaned from observing your colleagues.

5. Analysis: Explain how observing your colleagues has led to changes in your classroom teaching routines. Discuss how observing your colleagues enhanced/did not enhance your ability to grow as a teacher. Do you feel your suggestions have improved over time? Please refer to specific 2 + 2 suggestions you have made that you think were most helpful.

Teacher's Signature: _____   Date: _____

Principal's Signature: _____   Date: _____

appraisal would be a useful step in beginning to think of evaluation as a formative process. Teachers could begin to see assessment as a process of continuous improvement over which they have some control and input and for which they have responsibility."

"I really like the idea of self-evaluation as part of the appraisal process," said Joy thoughtfully. "Performance appraisal has always been something that's been done to teachers, not something that has encouraged real self-assess-ment. Self-assessment based on the feedback of teachers, administrators, and students sounds really powerful to me. As convinced as I am of the benefits of 2 + 2, getting the nuts and bolts of a workable program in place is still rather fuzzy to me. Do you have any suggestions about the practical considerations of developing a schoolwide 2 + 2 program?"

> 2 + 2 can be used to encourage teacher self-evaluation.

"Yes," said Dr. James, "you could have teachers agree to partici-pate on a voluntary basis, just as they have so far. To push the process further, simply ask those who are interested to formally sign up and commit to a reasonable number of observations each semester. That number can be negotiated, but I would caution against too low a number. Ten could be a reasonable minimum. With too few observa-tions, the real benefit of frequent feedback will erode.

"When 2 + 2 is first being implemented," he went on, "designat-ing a person to coordinate the program can be very helpful. Someone will need to orient the faculty, provide some initial training on the 2 + 2 protocol, and answer questions as they arise. Sissy would prob-ably allow some time for a teacher to serve in that role."

Dr. James thought for a moment before he continued. "I have one other suggestion of a practical nature. You could share copies of your respective schedules, so everyone could easily select the classes they wish to visit. It's too bad that the time for visiting teachers has to come out of your planning period, but maybe later you can convince Sissy to hire a substitute teacher from time to time. That way you wouldn't be cutting into your already inadequate planning time. You see, we don't want to create a big add-on program that will lose the battle with time. Even post-observation conferences should be at the discretion of the teacher. You said yourself they are happening in the most informal ways—at lunch or even in the hallways. Often a conference isn't necessary."

Joy expressed amazement that Dr. James seemed to anticipate her questions.

He laughed. "This isn't my first experience with a 2 + 2 implementation. The concerns you've brought up are fairly typical.

Just remember to keep it simple and observe often. I'd be pleased to hear from you again soon. Good luck! And please mention to Sissy that she is welcome to contact me with her questions at any time."

Joy left feeling well positioned to develop the next steps for 2 + 2 at Dewey High. *Now it's time to write up a proposal and visit Sissy,* she thought. She was anxious to share the powerful feedback the teachers had given in the 2 + 2 meeting. *How long,* she suddenly wondered, *has it been since anyone has given Sissy any praise?*

7

2 + 2

A Matter of Leadership

At its heart, the traditional view of leadership is based on assumptions of people's powerlessness, their lack of personal vision and inability to master the forces of change—deficits which can be remedied only by a few great leaders. The new view of leadership in learning organizations centers on subtler and more important tasks. In a learning organization, leaders are designers, stewards, and teachers. They are responsible for building organizations where people continually expand their capabilities to understand complexity, clarify vision, and improve shared mental models—that is, they are responsible for learning.

—Senge, 1990, p. 340

Although Joy had requested an appointment at one of the busiest times of the year, Sissy found time to meet with her. Sissy had plenty on her mind but felt she needed to hear how 2 + 2 was going. After all, she'd asked for feedback. The principals' meeting earlier in the week at the district office had increased her stress level greatly. The superintendent talked of nothing but accountability and test scores. At the same time, he urged principals to exercise leadership and take risks. But the message that came across was that anything short of success would not be tolerated. That made it a little difficult to consider anything risky. *What kind of leadership does he have in mind?* she wondered.

At least 2 + 2 doesn't involve much risk, Sissy thought. Perfectly low profile. She hadn't heard anything about 2 + 2 all semester and had all but forgotten it.

Joy was right on time as she stepped into Sissy's office.

"Hello, Joy, it's good to see you. Please have a seat and let's talk about 2 + 2."

"Thanks, Sissy," Joy replied, a little breathless after hurrying from her fourth floor classroom. "I've gotten a lot of positive feedback to report. Have you had a chance to read over my 2 + 2 proposal?"

"A written proposal? When did you give me that?" Sissy couldn't remember seeing a proposal from Joy. "Wait, let me check my inbox." A few moments later she had retrieved Joy's proposal. "I'm sorry," Sissy apologized. "It seems to have gotten buried! I promise to look it over as soon as I have time. Perhaps you can brief me on it now."

"I'd be happy to. Let me begin by giving you some of the data you requested at the beginning of the year about how teachers are reacting to 2 + 2." Joy reported on the meeting she'd had with the teachers and mentioned that twelve staff members had attended. "I was surprised how enthusiastic the teachers were," Joy related. "They were pleased at the feedback they received. Everyone seemed to have his or her own spin on why 2 + 2 was a great idea. Eventually some questions did come up, such as how to best fit 2 + 2 observations into the school day. We also discussed how to make suggestions. I guess their uncertainty is fairly predictable, since no one has had much experience giving feedback. Here are a few examples of 2 + 2 feedback teachers have given one another," Joy said, as she handed the printout to Sissy.

Joy paused as Sissy looked over the sample 2 + 2 feedback.

"I also visited Dr. James to get his feedback and to be sure that what we are doing with 2 + 2 is a reasonable approach," Joy continued as Sissy looked up again. "He suggested a reflection report that teachers could use to review and assess their experience with 2 + 2 observations and feedback. The reflection report is a self-assessment tool to help teachers process the value of the feedback they've received as well as the value of observing other classrooms. Teachers can also document any actions they have taken as a result, such as implementing a suggestion. He also pointed out that administrators and students could provide 2 + 2 feedback."

"I'm not sure administrators need to get involved," Sissy responded, "but teachers seem truly excited by the 2 + 2 idea." She noted that despite some uncertainty about making suggestions, teachers believed that 2 + 2 was exceptionally valuable. She hadn't anticipated that 2 + 2 would precipitate such a strong positive response.

"Some of the suggestions address lower level concerns," Sissy observed, "but I suppose sometimes that is helpful, too. I take it you're planning to continue with these 2 + 2 observations?"

"Definitely!" replied Joy. "That's what this proposal is all about. I would like to expand the program for next semester. You can see that 2 + 2 has already spread beyond our original group of four. Teachers feel that by having as many participants as possible it will be easier for them to schedule observations. Of course, that would also generate additional benefits by allowing teachers to see a wide range of teaching behaviors. But we'll need some lead time to let all the teachers know about 2 + 2. That's why I thought it would be useful to meet with you now to discuss details, rather than to wait until the end of the semester. Getting the word out early could really help teachers get involved during the spring semester.

Sissy was listening intently. "What do you have in mind?"

"Andy, Paige, and I were wondering if we could brief the entire staff on the 2 + 2 program before the upcoming holidays," Joy continued. "The next faculty meeting would provide a good opportunity, if there's room on the agenda. Teachers would have time to think about it before signing up in January. An orientation and training session could be scheduled then, and teachers could begin observations by mid-January."

"I have no objection to that," said Sissy. "Are you are willing to conduct an orientation and training session?"

> Teacher initiative and administrative support are both crucial to 2 + 2 success.

"I sure am!" replied Joy. "And I have some additional ideas about how best to organize the program."

"Joy, are these ideas in your proposal?" Sissy asked, as she stood up. "I'm running late for my next appointment, but I'd like to meet again after the next faculty meeting, just before vacation. I'll have had a chance to do my homework on your proposal by then. Go ahead, though, and make an announcement at the faculty meeting."

Joy was enthused. "I'll look forward to discussing the proposal with you before vacation then," she said as she left.

The day of the faculty meeting came quickly, and 2 + 2 had a place on the agenda. Joy, Andy, and Paige gave a presentation to the faculty about the merits of the 2 + 2 observations and fielded questions from the audience. It surprised Sissy that several teachers spoke out spontaneously in support of the program. She was beginning to realize that, although she hadn't initiated it, a peer observation program was taking shape. With so many daily crises and pressing issues, positive initiatives didn't always get her full attention.

She had finally gotten a chance to spend a few minutes reading Joy's proposal for implementing 2 + 2 during spring semester. She knew she was scheduled to discuss it with Joy the next day. After reading the proposal, Sissy also knew she was uncertain about how to respond.

The next day began with a couple of major discipline problems, so Sissy had no time to collect her thoughts before Joy arrived.

She began by saying, "I'm glad you're here, Joy, and I have read your proposal, but there have been so many distractions, it would be helpful if you would review for me just what you have in mind for next semester."

Joy jumped right in. "That's fine. I—we—would like this to be an official school program that includes the whole school. We've brainstormed a number of ways your support would be helpful. For example, organizing the program will take some time. I was going to propose that a free period be worked into the schedule, so a teacher could serve as program coordinator. It would be tremendously helpful if someone could be a point of contact to answer questions, meet with teachers, compile teachers' schedules to facilitate observations, and even to put together a handbook. I know how much time that takes because I did some of it myself this semester."

"I'm not able to respond to that right now, but I'll take it into consideration," Sissy said. "What else did you have in mind?"

"Based on what teachers had to say about 2 + 2," Joy continued, "I think it would be very helpful to have substitute teachers available to give teachers time to leave their classrooms. Then they wouldn't always have to sacrifice part of a planning period."

"Well, I don't know about that, either," said Sissy, recalling how this had concerned her when she first read the proposal. "Here we are getting into additional expense. I thought we were looking at 2 + 2 as a self-sustaining program—one that requires no extra budget."

"That's basically true," replied Joy. "But substitutes, especially at the beginning of the implementation, could help jump-start the program. You know, get teachers over the initial hurdle of leaving their classrooms. Substitutes could also provide some support for those who must always use planning time to observe. Time will always be an issue for teachers."

"I'll have to get back to you on this," replied Sissy. "Don't misunderstand," she added, "I do think 2 + 2 is a fine idea. But how much time and money can we invest in making it work?"

> Even an initiative that requires minimal resources to pilot needs additional resources if it is to become firmly established.

Joy swallowed hard. Sissy's interest so far had been encouraging, but she was definitely being cautious. Joy wanted her colleagues to consider 2 + 2 a priority, not simply a casual experiment. She decided to be completely candid.

"I think it's very important that we have as much support as possible. It's not just about extra time for planning or money for substitute teachers, although those things would help give 2 + 2 a fair chance to succeed. The program really needs an advocate like you. I very much value your acceptance of the 2 + 2 program so far. The staff and I consider ourselves fortunate that you are here at Dewey High. In fact, as I get to know you better, I find you both approachable and concerned about what teachers think. I'm just not sure most teachers have that perspective. It's nothing personal, Sissy," Joy assured her, "but you're an administrator. You are an unknown quantity to most of them. Some of them have a real problem with the order to produce an interdisciplinary unit, for example. When in doubt, they become defensive. Distrust of the administration could have a negative impact on their involvement with 2 + 2, a program that requires faith that the written feedback will have no adverse consequences for their futures at Dewey High. You could help dispel those fears by raising the profile of 2 + 2 and by letting everyone know you think it's a great program—with no risks involved for teachers.

"The reason I'm saying this," continued Joy, "is that I'm afraid many teachers, in spite of themselves, find performance appraisal observations threatening. We don't want this program to be colored by those perceptions. Trust is essential for 2 + 2 to work—trust among teachers and trust between administrators and teachers. If we show there's no hidden agenda here as far as you're concerned, teachers won't feel they're taking a risk by participating. I know how busy you are, but would it be possible for you to support 2 + 2 actively? For example, you could come to the orientation meeting, encourage participation, help answer questions, and reassure everyone that you really believe the process is valuable—and nonthreatening."

Sissy was quite unprepared for such candor. In fact, she was rather shocked. And she was stung by the implication that teachers might not be entirely comfortable around her. She felt teachers were happiest when they were left to concentrate on their classroom activities. For that reason, she had made no special effort to involve teachers in the affairs of the school and thought that the existing communication, though limited, was certainly adequate.

Joy apparently has some deeply felt convictions about this program, Sissy thought. *Isn't she just a little out of line, though?*

Sissy looked at Joy and spoke in measured tones. "Okay, Joy, I do see your point. Thanks for bringing your concerns into the open. I'm going to need some additional time to examine your proposal more closely and to determine how 2 + 2 can fit into the school's priorities. Even if I can't meet all your requests, however, I don't see that all is lost. Teachers can always visit one another's classrooms, if they so choose."

"Yes, I suppose that's true," Joy pushed. "But sometimes a program has to reach a critical mass of participants before it can have a really powerful effect. I have to think that the idea of every-one trying to do it on their own defeats the potential of a program designed to overcome isolation and maximize feedback."

> A critical mass is required for substantial change in the culture of the school.

Time to end this meeting, Sissy thought to herself. She stood up and said, "Again, thanks for sharing your thoughts. I'll be in touch."

Joy was downcast as she returned to her classroom. *What does it take to get the administration's support around here?* she wondered. This was a proposal that could only help teachers. And that was what Sissy was always talking about—improving teaching. Still, she worried that she had gone too far in her zeal. There wasn't much she could do about it now, though.

Alone in her office, Sissy found herself growing increasingly irritated. *I really need to clear my head,* she thought. *So much going on, and now this.* She picked up the phone and placed a call to Bill. "This is an SOS, Bill," she joked. "When are you going to be in the neighborhood again?"

"Coincidentally, I'm visiting a contractor near Dewey tomorrow morning," Bill replied. "Is there a problem?"

"Not exactly, but I could use a word or two of advice. How about lunch?" suggested Sissy.

"Fine. See you at noon."

Sissy was relieved to see Bill waiting for her at the local restaurant. After they were seated, she began to relate the details of her latest quandary.

"I just couldn't believe it," she related. "Joy wanted to have a free period, then have substitutes for teachers who wanted to do observations. Obviously, peer observation is something to encourage. But at the expense of other things? Incidentally, in her proposal she mentioned having 2 + 2 be incorporated into the performance appraisal system. Apparently, Dr. James has been involved in a program where 2 + 2 replaced the traditional performance appraisal system.

"Joy is absolutely convinced that the program has tremendous potential. She wants me to take it to the teachers and let them know it's a priority of mine. In fact, she was rather blunt in her assessment of the level of trust teachers hold toward me."

Sissy paused, not sure exactly what her question was. "I guess I'm trying to get on track with staff development for the curriculum changes I'd like to see, but I've been diverted by a program that the teachers seem to want. The few teachers who've participated do seem very excited by it. I feel like I'm going out on a limb, though, spending time and energy promoting it. Not to mention free periods and subs."

Bill nodded as she finished. "What do you really think about the program?" he asked.

"Well, peer observation does seem to have the potential to improve teaching, I suppose, but I'm not really sure how valuable it is in practice. I'm still wondering if teachers' comments can really make a difference in other teachers' performance."

"Does the performance appraisal system make a difference in their teaching?" asked Bill.

"Good point. Performance appraisal, as we've often discussed, doesn't seem to have any effect at all."

"Then maybe this is an opportunity to approach staff development from another angle," Bill suggested. "You've got nothing to lose, really. A free period is not a big deal, is it? I think even a token number of substitutes would help, too. Your sub bank is probably in pretty good shape. What I'm thinking is that if the program is properly supported, it may have a chance of bringing about real change. Collaboration among teachers could be stimulated—that, of course, would play right into your interdisciplinary efforts. But if you take a wait-and-see attitude, the whole initiative is likely to die on the vine. Teachers are awfully busy, too. Uncertainty about how you view the program will only leave teachers wondering why they should get involved."

"I hadn't thought about it that way at all," Sissy admitted. "Isn't it giving teachers a lot of free reign, though? If it's leadership

I'm supposed to be providing, how does this apply? This is entirely a teachers' initiative."

"Leadership can appear in many guises," Bill explained. "Sometimes it's hard to get over old notions about leadership. Directives aren't the only way to lead. While they have their place, the results you get are often a disappointment. If you really want people to change their beliefs and behaviors, you need to help them find reasons of their own to do so or give them the freedom to want to find reasons to change. The mission of a leader can be to promote growth by removing obstacles that limit growth. Perhaps that's your challenge at the moment."

"You mean, remove obstacles such as a lack of time? By offering a free period? I think I see where you're going, Bill," Sissy said thoughtfully. "Maybe, in a sense, I'm an obstacle—by not providing my support just because I'm not sure how the program will turn out."

"It's not a bad idea to take a risk now and again," Bill agreed.

"I'm so worried about the stance the district has taken with regard to accountability that I am a little on edge about anything different," Sissy conceded. "But how can anything change unless I get involved in making it happen?"

"Right. Improvement by accident rarely happens. At least here you're trying to design improvement by providing support for a peer feedback program. You know it won't go anywhere without you. If teachers continue to be excited about it, you may find it brings unexpected dividends. Trusting relationships are not to be underestimated, you know."

> Improvement by accident rarely happens.

They parted company with Sissy promising to keep Bill informed of her progress.

Later, as she reflected on their conversation, she realized how much it helped her to have a trusting relationship with someone at the district office. She felt empowered to take on new challenges. She felt indemnified against risk. Is this what the teachers needed from her in turn? She suddenly understood for the first time what Joy was trying to tell her.

Immediately after the December break, Sissy asked Joy to meet her in her office. "I've had time to consider your proposal in more depth," Sissy explained. "I'd like to offer as much support as I can. I think it's important to give 2 + 2 a fair chance to succeed. Otherwise, how will we know if it can make a difference?"

"You mean you've reconsidered the issue of a free period?" Joy asked.

"Exactly," replied Sissy. "Would you be willing to take responsibility for implementing the program? We can designate you the 2 + 2 Coordinator."

"I'd be happy to be the coordinator," exclaimed Joy. "Having sufficient time to devote to the 2 + 2 implementation is a big relief."

"Well, how about if you, Andy, and Paige form a 2 + 2 committee? The three of you did a nice job explaining the program at the last faculty meeting. They could help you assess the program and be available to provide support for teachers who have questions. There could be a committee report at faculty meetings, for example. That way, teachers could see that 2 + 2 is more than just your personal project. You would consult with the committee in your role as coordinator, and the committee would answer to me. Do you think that would be helpful?"

> A little support goes a long way to provide encouragement and promote forward momentum.

"That's a great idea, Sissy. I'll have to ask them, but I'm sure they'll be interested." Privately, Joy wondered what was going on. This was a first. The school didn't have many committees, and none of them had a professional agenda.

"I'm also looking into having substitute teachers cover classes for 2 + 2 teachers on occasion," Sissy continued. "It's a relatively low-cost way to show support. I'll review the sub days we have left soon—before the orientation meeting next week, in any case—and make a decision about how many we can afford."

"That's wonderful," Joy responded, still surprised at the turn of events. "I hope you'll be able to come to the orientation. Quite a lot of teachers have already mentioned their interest to me."

"I'll be there," said Sissy, "and I wouldn't mind having some time to talk to the teachers myself."

"That will be absolutely no problem!" Joy assured her.

Joy wanted to ask about 2 + 2 and performance appraisal but decided things were going so well at the moment that she didn't want to press her luck.

"Joy, there's one thing I need to ask of you," Sissy said. "I think you can see that I support this experiment. But I need you to follow through with your plans and be responsible for implementing this pilot. I simply don't have time to direct it. As I mentioned, I consider part of your task to be assessment of the program, especially now that you have some time. Please keep me informed of how everything is progressing."

"Thanks for placing your confidence in me, Sissy. I agree that it's important to assess what's going on with the 2 + 2 implementation. For one thing, I'll need to know when something's not working or needs adjustment. I'll be sure to keep you posted," Joy promised as she left the office.

The 2 + 2 orientation proved to be a useful session. Joy, as the program coordinator, reviewed the basis for the program and, using some of Dr. James's rationale, pointed out the value of feedback and encouragement. She mentioned the positive teacher responses to the initial observations in the fall.

George and Sara, two teachers who had already experimented with 2 + 2 observations, each conducted a short classroom demonstration, then asked for compliments and suggestions from everyone. Teachers shared their feedback as a group, so everyone could see the range of possibilities for compliments and suggestions. Gradually teachers relaxed as they saw that there were no right or wrong answers.

Joy continued with her briefing by reviewing all the concerns that had been raised at the first 2 + 2 meeting.

"This semester," she said, "I hope that the observations will be easier to accomplish. I have time during third period to organize the distribution of teachers' schedules and to experiment with how best to ensure a fairly equal distribution of visits among all participants. Your suggestions are welcome, of course. Sissy has asked Andy, Paige, and me to serve as a 2 + 2 committee, and we have agreed to do so. Again, with the help of your feedback, we can formalize some aspects of the program, such as the most appropriate number of observations to aim for each semester. Right now, we've agreed on ten, but when we have your input, that might change. You can bring any other concerns and suggestions to us, and we will continue to have regular meetings of 2 + 2 teachers. Sissy has also agreed to provide a limited number of substitutes on various days to help us find time to observe. I'll get more information about that to you later. Are there any questions?"

A number of questions were raised, reflecting some uncertainty among the teachers. "Who will see the comments?" asked one teacher. "Right," added another. "What if we don't agree with the criticisms we get? Can they be thrown out? How do we know that other teachers or the administration won't see them?"

"There is no requirement to act on any suggestion," Joy reminded them. "Only you can decide whether a comment is worthy of further attention. As for who will see the 2 + 2 forms, perhaps Sissy can help us with that." Surprisingly, that was an aspect of 2 + 2 that Joy hadn't recently considered.

Sissy, on the other hand, had given some thought to whether she wanted to see the feedback teachers were giving one another. "I am delighted," she began, "at the large number of you who are interested in volunteering to participate in 2 + 2. It shows the overwhelming commitment you have to improving as teachers. The more I learn about 2 + 2, the more convinced I am that you'll find it helpful and valuable. I'm also sensitive to the feelings of vulnerability you may have about exposing yourselves to the comments of others. I realize that some of the feedback may not always be completely accurate or relevant. Knowing this, I hope the time arrives when we trust each other enough that sharing the feedback is no longer an issue.

"For now, I won't need to see the individual 2 + 2 forms, if you don't feel comfortable sharing them with me. I will be visiting as many of you as I can and would be very willing to review your feedback with you to see how 2 + 2 is helping you or to consult on any plans you may have formed for implementing suggestions. However, whether you share them or not is entirely up to you, no strings attached." She paused so this information had a chance to sink in.

> Effective 2 + 2 requires regular visitations—both visiting and being visited.

"I feel strongly that 2 + 2 participants need to make a commitment to observe on a regular basis," Sissy continued. "I also expect everyone participating in 2 + 2 to complete a written reflection report at the end of the semester. You can see that you simply list the ten most valuable compliments and suggestions you've received and include the special insights or ideas you've picked up while observing your colleagues. Then, reflect on how the feedback has led to a change in your thinking, an improvement in your instruction, or plans to do things differently in the future. Remember, this means that only your input—your thoughts and reflections—will be submitted to me."

Sissy made sure no one had questions before continuing. "For those of you who are in your formal performance appraisal year, I would be happy to include your participation in 2 + 2 as evidence that you've exceeded the professional activities standard. Your reflection report can be attached to your formal performance appraisal and become part of your permanent record. You may also want to use your 2 + 2 feedback to document your peer observation. As you may recall, the district offers recertification points for peer observation. I would suggest that all of you make the reflection report a part of your professional teacher portfolio. 2 + 2 is an excellent way to show what you've learned and how you have grown, and that's definitely a significant part of demonstrating your professionalism. I'm confident that as 2 + 2 gets underway, your concerns about sharing the feedback you've received will disappear pretty quickly. It's much more fun than it is scary. Here's to a successful semester!"

The teachers were silent for a moment and then broke into spontaneous applause. Later, back in her office as she reflected on the session, Sissy felt elated at the encouragement she had received at the meeting.

8

2 + 2 Takes Off

Mistakes are, after all, the foundations of truth, and if a man does not know what a thing is, it is at least an increase in knowledge if he knows what it is not.

—Carl Jung (1875–1961)

The semester began to pick up momentum almost immediately, and the observations quickly became part of the routine at Dewey High. Sissy hired two substitute teachers to free fourteen teachers for observation sessions. The substitute teachers rotated among the fourteen classrooms so that each substitute taught for a different classroom teacher during each of the seven daily teaching periods. The following week, three substitute teachers permitted more than twenty teachers to complete two observations. Sissy couldn't supply substitute teachers for every observation, but she decided she could afford one substitute every two weeks. Teachers knew that wasn't ideal but appreciated the efforts to protect their planning time. Once teachers had gotten their feet wet, they didn't hesitate to use their planning period when necessary. Joy discovered many of them actually preferred to be able to visit their colleagues on the spur of the moment rather than commit themselves to a substitute's schedule ahead of time.

Joy was greatly encouraged by the feedback and anecdotes she received from her colleagues. As she reported to Sissy in one of their hallway encounters, "Now that everyone's gotten started, it seems teachers are much less concerned about how their colleagues view them. That's the magic of compliments, I guess."

"Yes, indeed," Sissy responded, "I'm pleased at the way teachers are breaking down some of the barriers that cause isolation."

"That reminds me," said Joy, "a couple of teachers have asked whether they can visit the middle school for 2 + 2 observations. A foreign language teacher, for instance, wants to look in on some eighth-grade classes before the students move up here to the high school. She thinks better coordination might be possible as a result."

Sissy hadn't ever considered that idea but was elated to learn teachers were thinking up new ways to collaborate. "They'll have to contact the teachers they want to visit ahead of time, of course," she said. "But I see no problem with it—the middle school is right next door. I'd be happy to speak with the principal about it if you think that would be useful." Joy thought that would be very helpful, so Sissy promised to see to it.

> 2 + 2 observations of teachers in other subjects and other grade levels are often as useful as observations of a teacher's own subject area or grade level.

Another teacher, Barry, was particularly happy about an experience he'd had with 2 + 2. He told Joy how he'd been hoping to observe Bea, whom he considered to be a master teacher. Bea wasn't participating in 2 + 2, but she had seen Barry visiting other teachers' classrooms and was curious about it. Barry was persistent in his requests and eventually Bea agreed to be observed. Afterward, she agreed to observe Barry's classroom during her planning period. Since then, she had even taken over Barry's class twice—with Barry observing. "I guess you might call it a kind of minicoaching relationship," Barry said.

Joy found that most teachers echoed the many enthusiastic comments from the program's initial 2 + 2 group. One said, "I think in the short time we've been doing 2 + 2 here at Dewey High, I've learned more from my colleagues than I have in a multitude of inservices. The comments they have written have given me more insight, so I can see the whole picture. Some teachers have focused on the smaller details that I might often overlook."

Another teacher reported, "I think I've actually learned more going to someone else's class than having someone observe me. That's a very big advantage of 2 + 2, and it only confirms what I've always believed: We have an excellent group of teachers here. I think we have the best of the best. This has also been a great kind of support because no one ever told me in the past that I was doing such a good job. I'm enjoying this!"

"When 2 + 2s were being done on me, I read the suggestions and thought, 'Okay, this is good. Maybe I need some improvement in this area.' Then I thought about my first performance appraisal, and I recalled that it just said I needed to improve. It didn't really focus on something specific I was doing. When I go to observe another teacher, 2 + 2 forces me to offer specific suggestions on how the teacher I'm visiting can improve. I also ask myself, 'How can I learn from this teacher?' I've never viewed myself as evaluating another teacher. I've always seen myself going into that room and learning from that teacher."

Teachers also had advice for each other on how to react to unexpected comments. "Focus on not getting defensive," suggested one teacher. "One observer totally missed what I was doing, and I got really defensive. I was going to go tell the person off, but then I thought, 'Wait, if what I was doing wasn't obvious enough, maybe I should be doing something differently.'"

Another teacher reacted with good humor rather than becoming defensive. "Somebody did a 2 + 2 on me once. Just before she came in, a different teacher sent two misbehaving eleventh graders to my class of ninth graders. I used them as referees and the 2 + 2 teacher wrote, 'Those two referees are sure causing a commotion!' I didn't feel the need to go to the teacher and explain what was happening. But about a week later, I saw her in the hall, and we had a good laugh over it."

Joy found that nearly all the 2 + 2 teachers were still sometimes at a loss when it came to making suggestions. "I'm still having some difficulty coming up with two suggestions on every visit," said Andy at the first of the 2 + 2 spring semester meetings. "From some of the observation forms I receive with only one or sometimes no suggestions, I see I'm not the only one."

"Sometimes we're not sure where to start," George, a music teacher, added.

"Maybe we could focus on particular areas," someone suggested. "There are different sources that document teacher skills that we might look at."

> Teaching standards, frameworks for teaching, or the evaluation domains from more traditional appraisal systems can be used to cue topics for compliments and suggestions in 2 + 2 observations.

"What about just a list of the domains or categories in the traditional performance appraisal?" suggested Terry. "It would give us some idea of specific areas to observe. It wouldn't be a requirement to address any of the areas, but it could make us more aware of possible things to consider."

The suggestion met with general agreement. "Later, we could develop our own kind of cheat sheet from other sources," added Sara.

"Or we could tailor the specific areas to focus on some things our department wants to highlight."

"I have a feeling some of us could use help formulating the suggestions themselves," commented Barry.

"That's probably true," said Terry. "Some of the feedback I'm getting is excellent, and some is pretty generic. I've had some prior experience observing and giving feedback and so has Bea. Maybe we can set up a little presentation and then answer questions from any of you who are interested in coming." Many teachers thought that this would be helpful.

"Thanks for your offer, Terry," said Joy. "Let me know when you want to schedule your session. And, everyone, don't be too hard on yourselves. The quality of your suggestions is improving as we gain experience. We're all getting better at this! Would it help if I circulated a list of actual suggestions—minus your names? It might give us a better perspective on how the program is going."

Joy's suggestion met with immediate approval.

Possible Categories for 2 + 2 Observation Focus

1. Use of Technical Skills

> Reinforcement
>
> Questions
>
> Examples
>
> Teaching aids
>
> Lesson structure
>
> Group learning

2. Pedagogical Skills

> Effective preparation
>
> Learner attention
>
> Learner interest

3. Course Content

> Clearly identified concepts
>
> Clear distinction between concepts and illustrations
>
> Appropriate level of complexity

4. Classroom Management

   Variety of control techniques

   – Positive and negative
   – Verbal and nonverbal

   Efficiency of class administration

   Use of students in administrative tasks

5. Trial-and-Error Learning

   Appreciation of mistakes

   Openness to student correction

   Sufficient repetition

6. Classroom Environment

   Joy

   Order

   Best use of facility

7. Language Skills

   Clear pronunciation

   Good vocabulary level

   Effective communication

8. Evaluation

   Modification in lessons based on real-time experience

   Awareness of learners' success or failure

   Assistance to weak students

9. Administrative Issues

Sissy, who was present during the last part of the meeting, was generally pleased with the progress. Teachers were discovering new skills, and she was discovering a few things herself. Andy, for example, was no longer lecturing the entire class period. She had paid him a 2 + 2 visit and had seen him skillfully facilitate a discussion with highly engaged students. When she left, she checked Andy's performance appraisal file for her predecessor's report. Sure enough, her predecessor had made comments similar to hers about Andy's teaching style. He hadn't changed much in years, until now. She smiled. This made her job a whole lot easier.

Sissy had also discovered how much the teachers appreciated her feedback when she wasn't involved in a rating process. A feeling of trust was being built, and Sissy was enjoying it. Her burden was much lighter. Her faculty somehow seemed more alive. And she didn't seem to have to push nearly as hard. She didn't know it yet, but some ideas were beginning to form in her mind to lighten her burden even further.

Sissy was not entirely without concerns about 2 + 2, however. She had invested some time and energy into supporting the program, an effort for which she had received no feedback from her own supervisors. She was also still struggling with her staff development plans. How could 2 + 2 fit into the larger scheme of school goals and district concerns? What about the suggestion Sara had made to create a focus for 2 + 2 observations based on departmental objectives? Was there really a way that 2 + 2 could serve as a more formal performance appraisal function? She decided that she was overdue for a consultation with Dr. James.

Sample of Dewey High School
Teachers' 2 + 2 Suggestions

- "You may want to have a conference with the few students who seem to be less interested."
- "Could a student introduce the vocabulary?"
- "Encourage all students to participate in group activities."
- "I bet this would work equally well in small groups."
- "Do you ever praise the group that finishes an exercise first and has the most accurate results?"
- "What about a word game with the present perfect?"
- "Maybe one of the students could have led the class in going over the homework."
- "Slow down! You cover a lot in a little bit of time. Give the students time to digest."
- "When I taught this level course, I found it helpful to base the students' grades heavily on class participation. Getting them to do what they need to is our most difficult task here."
- "When you are reviewing the warm-up, you might break down the steps of the problem and involve more students (e.g., What is the first step? Find the lowest common denominator. What is the LCD?)."
- "It might be a good idea to keep the door closed to avoid disruptions."
- "Do you have a syllabus or just verbally state the objectives? You may want to write them for the visually oriented students."
- "Colored chalk helps students focus on important info!"
- "Ask students to clarify, revise, and justify responses."
- "Have you considered using more visuals or multimedia?"
- "Encourage speakers to present a summary of part of the newspaper article instead of reading aloud selected paragraphs."

9

Beyond the 2 + 2 Basics

A Second Interlude

Reality leaves a lot to the imagination.

—John Lennon (1940–1980)

It was a Monday morning in late April, and Sissy was sitting in Dr. James's office at the university. She was satisfied that teachers were benefiting tremendously from participating in 2 + 2. And it seemed that the teachers themselves were really excited. But she was looking beyond the current semester. Sissy was goal oriented, and she was wondering if and how 2 + 2 might develop further.

"Yes, indeed," Dr. James explained, "there's quite a wide range of possible applications of 2 + 2. How it actually develops is up to you and your faculty. Of course, the more opportunities for teachers to observe teaching, the better perspective they'll have on the whole elephant. And teachers sharing expertise naturally leads to more shared knowledge. Thus, teachers themselves help raise the collective level of the profession by utilizing an ever-expanding range of teaching expertise."

"It all makes sense to me," Sissy said, "especially in theory. But I have some questions about 2 + 2 in practice. Visiting other teachers in other departments and grade levels—and even in different schools—is very interesting in an exploratory kind of way. But I would like to look into exactly how teachers can get the most benefit from observing each other."

"Exploratory ways are absolutely necessary at times," Dr. James assured her. "Teachers can gain an amazing amount of knowledge by randomly observing teachers from different subject areas and grade levels. But I think I understand your question. There should be freedom to explore with 2 + 2, yet many possibilities for focusing 2 + 2 observations exist as well.

"It all depends on what you intend to accomplish. If the purpose is for teachers to be exposed to a wide variety of perspectives about teaching in general, there is less need to prioritize the categories of teaching behaviors during classroom observations. On the other hand, is there a school-wide goal you're working toward, or a new program you would like to implement? Is there a particular teaching behavior to which each observer should be alert when giving feedback? In that case, guidelines explaining the priorities for compliments and suggestions would be appropriate."

> A single set of priorities for 2 + 2 observations may be agreed on for all feedback throughout the school; at other times, the focus of the 2 + 2 observation may be left to the initiative of the individual teacher. Both approaches to feedback are useful.

"That certainly makes sense," Sissy agreed.

"Would some teachers like to set their own goals to improve instruction?" Dr. James asked. "They could then ask observers to prioritize their 2 + 2 feedback based on those goals. Teachers might even pair up for a time to develop a mutual coaching relationship. 2 + 2 can be varied, serving individual needs and schoolwide goals. But no matter what shape 2 + 2 takes, the key is still frequent, specific, feedback, preferably from a variety of sources."

"It's interesting that you mention 2 + 2 serving schoolwide needs," Sissy commented. "The biggest concern I have is staff development. I have tried, with limited success, to encourage teachers to expand their teaching strategies and approaches to curriculum. For example, I asked every teacher to develop at least one interdisciplinary unit last year. I have no idea how many of them actually did it, but I had a consultant come in to give a workshop. Interdisciplinary teaching requires many different skills to be effective. It's kind of overwhelming—and I know that a few presentations from experts aren't going to transform anyone's teaching. I'm getting a lot of resistance—mostly passive resistance. When the classroom door closes, it's business as usual, I'm afraid."

"You couldn't be more right about that," Dr. James agreed.

"The interesting thing is that I've seen a couple of instances where a teacher is doing something differently because of a 2 + 2 suggestion," Sissy continued. "I've also seen many excellent suggestions. But there's a wide range of quality among the comments I've seen. Many of them are very general, and quite a few are really not very useful. So I'm really interested in how 2 + 2 can be better focused. And I'd like to know how 2 + 2 can help with my other initiatives, such as interdisciplinary teaching."

"One of the keys to solving your staff development problems is your own realization that a few workshops aren't enough," replied Dr. James. "Let me try to explain how 2 + 2 can support your goals and initiatives. Let's take the example of your interdisciplinary initiative. With the help of your teachers or a teacher committee, your interdisciplinary initiative could be broken into several specific categories. One such category might answer the question, has the context for a particular lesson been broadened to encompass multiple disciplines? How? Or has the teacher developed ways to achieve objectives through collaborative approaches? How? The list could go on and on. It all depends on what you and your staff consider important.

"At any rate, once the relevant categories have been established, your teachers would then be asked to give priority to the agreed-on areas when conducting 2 + 2 observations. Each teacher would know what the established priorities were and would expect the observer to offer suggestions and recognize achievements in those skill areas. You might even have a number of teachers form staff development study groups focused on a specific skill. Later, these groups might also offer other faculty members informal training sessions on those skills."

"I wonder how difficult that would be to organize," Sissy said thoughtfully. "Even if it took some time, we'd gain focus on a common goal and have a roadmap to follow. What other options do you see?"

"Another possibility, as I mentioned, would be to begin with individual teachers," Dr. James responded. "Teachers could establish their own goals for improvement in relation to the schoolwide plan. Each 2 + 2 observer would then direct his or her feedback to these preestablished goals.

"Or, under your guidance, each department or grade level might develop its own set of priorities in support of your interdisciplinary initiative. Teachers might also identify other areas of opportunity within the department or grade level. For example, the science department might be trying to implement inquiry-based learning in conjunction with an interdisciplinary curriculum. Science teachers might commit half of their 2 + 2 observations to other department members and half to others in the school. Teachers from other departments could receive guidelines from the science teachers and prioritize their feedback to focus on inquiry-based learning when observing in the science department. You can see that the possibilities for 2 + 2 to support school goals are nearly infinite. Your job is to clarify and continually communicate the agreed-on objectives. You'll also find it helpful, of course, to continue to make your own 2 + 2 visits to teachers."

> Teachers may ask observers to check on specific aspects of instruction. When this happens, it is still important to balance both compliments and suggestions.

As she listened, Sissy's head began to fill with new ideas. And 2 + 2 definitely had a role to play. "This is really very interesting," she exclaimed. "I don't know why I didn't see it myself. The one thing you said that caught me off guard, though, was your comment about my own 2 + 2 visits. I guess I haven't been as conscientious about that as I should be. But if what goes on in each teacher's classroom is what really matters, I need to be actively involved. With 2 + 2, it's easier to give compliments and suggestions than it is to critique a teacher as part of a formal performance appraisal.

"But I'm still concerned about the quality of some teachers' suggestions," Sissy added. "Actually, the teachers have made plans for those with more experience, such as the department heads, to hold sessions on developing critical observation skills. They also have occasional meetings where they air and share their concerns and problems with the program. Nevertheless, I guess I'm still tied to the performance appraisal system. I just want to be sure the standards are high enough . . ."

"Your point is well taken," replied Dr. James. "The quality of feedback does become important, especially over the long term. But so far, nothing has been lost, and everything gained, including a confidence on the teachers' part that they have something to offer other teachers. If I understand you correctly, your teachers already feel they have gained much from 2 + 2. You know, sometimes even feedback that appears trivial can have a salutary effect on performance. Perhaps most important, the element of trust that has developed will pave the way for the acceptance of more specific and critical feedback in the future."

"I'm glad you understand my concern," Sissy smiled. "How do we move forward from here?"

"The good news is that your 2 + 2 teachers are already asking for help with suggestions, Sissy. The sessions planned by teachers who offered to share their expertise in observation and feedback techniques will undoubtedly enhance the value of 2 + 2. Since your teachers feel that their 2 + 2 meetings are useful to them, I would suggest that you encourage them by arranging time for meetings during school hours, if possible. In this way, teachers can improve their feedback skills by discussing their problems and successes with their 2 + 2 observations. You get the picture, I'm sure."

"Yes, of course, but are you sure that's going to be enough?" asked Sissy.

Dr. James smiled. "Enough in what way? As you think about this, you may want to revise how your standards are defined. What was so wonderful about performance appraisal feedback? Was it uniformly useful and accurate? Wasn't it also the form and the schedule that made it seem objective and standardized? The benefits of 2 + 2 should be visible to teachers and administrators. The self-assessment should give plenty of evidence of growth. And classroom observations should reveal improvements in teaching behaviors. This is more than can be said for most performance appraisal systems. A teacher who does everything right according to an appraisal system can still be a pretty mediocre teacher."

"I have to agree, Dr. James," Sissy said thoughtfully. "As a matter of fact, I'm slowly changing the way I think about performance appraisal. As long as we're on the subject, I wanted to discuss the issue of 2 + 2 as a formal performance appraisal alternative."

Sissy hadn't forgotten the feedback Joy had shared with her last semester. "Teachers wanted to know if 2 + 2 could become our performance appraisal program," Sissy explained. "Since performance appraisal is strictly a district policy matter, all I can do is mention 2 + 2 participation on a teacher's traditional professional appraisal summary. But I'm wondering how valid such an idea might be. If 2 + 2 brings actual change in teacher practice, isn't it already accomplishing more than a traditional appraisal?"

"Excellent point, Sissy," Dr. James agreed. "Much of the value of feedback lies in receiving it regularly, if not continuously. The timing, content, frequency, and follow-up to feedback are all important. Under the traditional appraisal system, feedback is infrequent. Sometimes years are spent teaching with no feedback from another adult.

"Teachers are not against evaluation but are not happy with inappropriate evaluation. You've probably noticed that teachers don't buy

> Teachers are not against evaluation but are not happy with evaluation that doesn't give help and support.

in to the traditional evaluation process when they perceive that it is geared toward identifying incompetent staff. Administrators do have important roles in identifying marginal teachers, organizing professional assistance, and, if necessary, arranging plans of action. But they also have important contributions to make when offering feedback to competent teachers."

"I'm well aware that teachers are dissatisfied with the typical performance appraisal process. To be honest, I'm not very comfortable with it myself," admitted Sissy.

"And understandably so," said Dr. James. "When teachers are to be rated in a summative assessment, administrators are expected to be experts in every subject area, experts in pedagogy, and sensitive to all performance obstacles. They cannot, however, be all things to all people and are set up to fail when their main purpose—performing a task perceived as disagreeable by many administrators and teachers alike—becomes issuing a rating once every several years."

"That's for sure!" exclaimed Sissy. "But how can 2 + 2, which seems to be such a rich professional development tool, also be used for performance appraisal?"

"That's an interesting question, Sissy," Dr. James replied. "First, assessment and professional development cannot be separated. Any type of professional growth involves critical judgment of some aspect of the act of teaching. At the same time, assessment that neglects clear, specific, and ongoing feedback relative to both positive accomplishments and areas for improvement is relatively meaningless. Summative evaluations themselves are not at issue here. They can serve a useful purpose and contribute to professional development. It is the model of summative evaluation that emphasizes ratings and offers little feedback to improve instruction that is outmoded.

"Second, the goal of evaluation for teachers already in the acceptable range should be to improve instruction. But in traditional evaluation systems, ratings, not feedback, become the main objective. In the environment of summative assessments every few years, teachers are understandably cautious. Situations that further limit opportunities for learning may be created.

> In traditional evaluation systems, ratings, not feedback, become the main objective.

For example, when teachers set goals as part of the appraisal process, they are likely to identify areas of strength rather than weakness to minimize risk. Yet growth depends on taking risks, trying new approaches, and experimenting—behavior not encouraged by the traditional appraisal approach. And what is the purpose of assessment when it does not lead to growth or improvement?"

"I never thought that the purpose of a goal-setting strategy was to minimize risk," Sissy remarked. "Could that mean the appraisal process might actually serve as a disincentive for improvement of teaching?"

"For some teachers, that's certainly a possibility," Dr. James agreed. "That's another way 2 + 2 can help. 2 + 2 reduces the perceived risk of making changes in teaching practice and offers support through peer feedback. Additionally, teachers see other teachers taking the same kinds of risks. We haven't talked much about the process from the viewpoint of the observer. As evidence from the 2 + 2 program implementation indicates, teachers get powerful feedback about teaching performance by acting as observers as well as by being observed. The experience of observing another professional model different strategies is rare in the teaching world, and it enlarges perspectives. I've heard at least one 2 + 2 teacher speak of the 2 + 2 program in terms of tearing down walls. At the same time, teachers must engage in critical judgment while writing compliments and suggestions—an exercise that can lead to greater awareness of the observing teacher's own strengths and weaknesses; that is, the act observing can be coupled with self-assessment.

"So you see, 2 + 2 serves both assessment and professional development objectives very well. It would be interesting if you were able to persuade the district to allow an exemption from the traditional appraisal process for Dewey High. You would probably need to document the progress your teachers make under the 2 + 2 program, but that would be a good idea anyway."

"It all makes so much sense. There are so many ways 2 + 2 can support professional development and assessment and serve the school's goals, too," Sissy said with enthusiasm. "I have some planning to do."

"You've accomplished a lot already!" Dr. James reassured her.

Back at her office, Sissy recalled the other uses of 2 + 2 that Dr. James had casually suggested. She could start a whole culture of

> The real payoff comes when we establish a culture of 2 + 2 in the school.

2 + 2 in the school by requesting 2 + 2 feedback for faculty inservices, faculty meetings, or for any meeting. Student 2 + 2s, parent 2 + 2s, and even 2 + 2s on administrators could be considered.

When she had protested that she would collapse under all the feedback she would no doubt receive once teachers had the opportunity to do 2 + 2s on administrators, Dr. James had laughed. "Simply toss feedback that is useless, or already known, into the trash," he said, "and highlight anything useful for future reference."

How could she address the concerns of the Dewey High staff if she didn't know what they were? How could she make use of her teachers' expertise if she didn't have their suggestions? Wasn't it better to know than not to know? "Besides," he had remarked, "positive feedback is always energizing."

She had to agree with that. Dr. James had certainly given her lots of encouragement for her support of the 2 + 2 program at Dewey High. And she was already developing a very clear picture of the evolution of both 2 + 2 and staff development next semester. Sissy decided to cancel the guest speaker for the last faculty inservice day in May. She could better use that time to develop a plan with her staff.

10

Institutionalizing 2 + 2

A little knowledge that acts is worth infinitely more than much knowledge that is idle.

—Kahlil Gibran (1883–1931)

Later that week, the Dewey High 2 + 2 teachers came together for their third after-school 2 + 2 meeting of the semester. These informal get-togethers were held every four weeks or so. At the first meeting near the end of February, a few teachers surprised the group with pizza. Now refreshments were an integral component of each meeting. As had happened during the first semester, teachers continued asking nonparticipating teachers if they would visit their classrooms to conduct 2 + 2 observations. Usually it didn't take long for the nonparticipating teachers to venture out to observe someone else. Now, as April drew to a close, nearly 75% of the faculty had conducted at least one 2 + 2 observation, and a large cross-section of both new and relatively experienced 2 + 2 teachers came together at the meetings.

As the semester progressed, the focus shifted from logistical issues about 2 + 2 to questions of instruction and classroom management. Teachers had become quite comfortable with each other. Some even shared specific bits of feedback they had received. Discussion then centered on key areas of concern. One time the topic was how

> As 2 + 2 matures, the focus often shifts from logistical issues to questions of instruction and classroom management.

best to involve apathetic students. Another time someone sought help for a collaborative learning experiment that had turned chaotic. A couple of times, teachers shared new ideas they had tested out in their classrooms. At this meeting, Barry commented that he had his students help create their own tests. Others immediately wanted to know the details. The discussion quickly became a debate on how much student input was prudent.

As the 2 + 2 coordinator, Joy was always looking for new perspectives on the program that she could bring up for discussion. One idea she brought up for discussion at a past meeting was coaching relationships: Two or more teachers could choose to coach each other on a specific teaching element, limiting their visits for a time to members of their small group.

Today, Joy wanted to revisit student 2 + 2s. Student 2 + 2s were not an official part of the program agreed to by teachers in January, and reception to this idea had been distinctly lukewarm thus far. Yet Joy fully appreciated Dr. James's emphasis on the importance of student feedback. Why rely solely on the use of indirect feedback, inferred through test scores? Surely students had some meaningful input regarding what did and did not work well in the classroom. After all, who were the ultimate intended beneficiaries of all this teaching expertise? The students, of course.

She'd heard many objections: "Maybe with my advanced math classes they'd have some good feedback, but I don't see how my general math class would have any input" and "There are a few of the better students I could ask, but the majority of them would be clueless."

Joy had also heard objections based on the opinion that the school's student population was too challenged to take anything like student 2 + 2s seriously. Some teachers implied that students would have a field day with something like 2 + 2 and use it as a license for open season on teachers. With all the negative comments, Joy wanted to ask whether anyone had actually experimented with student 2 + 2s.

She found she didn't need to raise the topic at all. Barry's discussion about student-created tests triggered feedback from a small group of teachers who related, with some enthusiasm, how they'd gotten started with student 2 + 2s.

Bea advised tact. "It's important how you say it. Focus not on two things you like about me but two things you like about the class. It takes the focus off of you, and they're amazed you actually want to know what they think. They'll come up with a genuine response. I use it quite a bit, and an off-the-wall response is very rare."

Another teacher agreed. "My student 2 + 2s are especially useful when I want to implement something different. It motivates them to improve, too."

"That's exactly right," exclaimed Anita. "I'll let students know I'm going to try something and that I'm going to ask for their 2 + 2 feedback afterwards. If most of the class like it and have only minor suggestions for fine-tuning, great! If not, we use the suggestions to fix it—or simply throw it out. They're usually very good with their comments. They'll say, 'Oh, no, don't throw it away' and really come through with ways to solve the problem. It's a game, and they love games. 'We can do it a second time and do it better.'"

"Didn't students take advantage of 2 + 2 to say irresponsible things?" Carla wanted to know.

"Not so far," Darren responded. "It helps if the teacher makes the class atmosphere conducive to suggestions. I purposely make mistakes from time to time, and when the kids correct me I say, 'Oh, thanks very much.' They're actually more sensitive than a lot of adults. If they have to correct me, most of the time they'll do it very professionally."

"You know," added Andy, "I think it gives them a sense of ownership. They know they are being listened to and that their ideas can impact the classroom. The quality of their comments improves with practice, too."

"My concern is the need to process feedback from twenty-five or thirty-five students. That's a lot of work!" remarked an English teacher who already had plenty of written work to review.

"Well, if you really wanted to make it quick," answered Andy, "couldn't you just skim them, keep any useful comments, and throw away the rest?"

"Right! And sometimes those few comments are extremely useful," added Joy. "One of my students wondered if she could teach a class lesson on her research topic, rather than just turning in her report. After setting guidelines, I let several students do that, and it was really successful. It reminded me that no matter how well we think we're teaching, the bottom line is how the students are doing."

"Speaking of student performance, my students liked the idea one of them suggested of preparing for a test with a study buddy during class," added Paige. "They enjoy the interaction with each other, and, as long as I define specific objectives, they stay on task, too."

"You know, isn't this kind of reflection something that's educational in itself?" asked Terry. "We want them to think about what they're doing, not just memorize the lesson. As Andy mentioned, they also gain some ownership, which is one way to help them make a connection with the real world of active learning."

"The other thing I've noticed," added Sara, "is that students have begun to comment on the fact that teachers are helping each other out by observing classes. They think it's kind of cool that teachers still have something to learn. I think 2 + 2 helps us model the idea that learning continues for everyone, no matter how old and gray you get."

"I know we've talked a lot about student feedback here," said Paige, "but I'm still wondering about giving feedback to each other. I'm looking forward to Bea and Terry's session on observational skills. But what about the focus of the observation feedback? The sheet 'Possible Categories for 2 + 2 Observation Focus' is useful, but there are so many categories. I would like to develop a more specific focus relevant to our school goals. We talked about this a couple of months ago."

"Well, in our department," interjected Sara, "there are particular things we'd like to focus on since we're implementing a new math series. Maybe we need to identify separate elements of the program, prioritize them, and be able to choose which ones to focus on during observations. Teachers outside the math department might find this type of list helpful when they visit math teachers, too." Many heads nodded in agreement.

"Maybe it's time to expand our approach," said Joy. "Our session on observation and feedback skills and this idea of observations focusing on certain school or department initiatives really bridge over into staff development. 2 + 2 could serve several purposes. Perhaps I could discuss it with Sissy and see how to organize this."

"Remind her the administrators are supposed to be doing 2 + 2, too," someone called from the rear of the room. "I haven't seen her all year!"

"It would be good if administrators were more involved," Terry agreed. "And if students are doing 2 + 2s on us, why not teachers observing administrators and offering them our 2 + 2 comments?" Not many teachers had thought of this before, but there was a murmur of agreement. "In all seriousness, she's missing out on a lot!"

Joy hadn't thought of that before either but realized immediately that Sissy *was* indeed losing out on both compliments and suggestions. "Great idea," she said.

Joy could see time was up. "One last thing—I've got a survey here about the 2 + 2 program. All of your feedback is really important, so please take a few moments to fill it out and return it by the end of next week. I'll have the results by our last meeting in June."

As she passed out the survey, Joy was pleased with all the sharing that was going on at Dewey High. After nearly everyone had left, she sat down with Paige and Andy to briefly outline their next meeting with Sissy.

The three of them were eager to make their case for a more focused approach to 2 + 2. Connecting observations to specific initiatives in their own departments, they felt, was a way to further validate the potential of 2 + 2. Improvement would be supported in a way that Sissy could surely appreciate. In addition, they definitely wanted to address the performance appraisal issue. Could an experimental program using 2 + 2 as performance appraisal be piloted at Dewey High? More than likely, if Sissy were open to the concept, she would know how to approach the district office.

———————————————

In her office that day, Sissy was meeting with Bill. He had been advising one of her assistant principals regarding a new technology opportunity for the school. After he briefed Sissy on the status of the project, he turned the conversation toward her 2 + 2 "problem."

"I've been hearing some interesting things from teachers about this 2 + 2 program," he said. "I understand you've given them quite a bit of support. It's become kind of high profile around here, far as I can see. How do you think it's going?"

"I can tell you that it's surprised me in some ways," Sissy conceded. "I've learned a lot about the teachers on this staff. Given the opportunity to learn from one another, they've shown themselves to be extremely serious about improving their teaching. Teachers seem to be trying out different strategies, and I've seen for myself many positive changes in the way they interact with students.

> Given the opportunity to learn from one another, teachers become extremely serious about improving their teaching.

"And that's always good news," responded Bill. "How are you feeling about your school improvement plans?"

"I'm taking another look at how to go about it," Sissy replied. "I'm not as frustrated by teachers' resistance to any change. Maybe the problem was the approach I was taking. Frankly, teachers seem quite open to new ideas under the right circumstances. The more I take a collaborative approach, like supporting their 2 + 2 initiative, the better the response I get. I think 2 + 2 gives them the chance to be a part of the inquiry process. Some new collaboration among the teachers is taking place as a result of observing one another, by the way—just as you predicted. And," she added, "the concept of continuous improvement now has some basis in reality. Everyone pays lip service to continuous improvement, and in reality there's never been any vehicle for frequent assessment. The ongoing observations all semester, though, provide the opportunity for regular, frequent self-assessment.

"I'm planning to try to incorporate 2 + 2 observations in more specific ways into the schoolwide curricular improvement plans. I had a talk with Dr. James, and he provided a number of ideas to make the most out of teacher feedback. It's not a silver bullet, of course, but I'm actually getting pretty excited about its potential to stimulate real change."

"You know, I'm really glad you had the foresight to encourage these observations," Bill said. "It's amazing what happens when teachers have the chance to shed their isolation. I'd say it could also have a positive impact on the professionalization of teaching. The bottom line, of course, is whether this professional interaction also impacts student achievement. Cause and effect when it comes to student achievement is very hard to measure. But if you could manage a way to assess the program's effects, I'd be very interested in your conclusions. I'm convinced that the program has potential for districtwide implementation."

Sissy was extremely gratified by his remarks. "Actually a teacher-led 2 + 2 committee is in place, and part of their task is to assess the program. But I will offer them some assistance on how best to go about it. I agree that it's very important to know how it affects the school so that we can think about disseminating the program. But right now, I already know that it is making a difference, and that's enough for me."

"This is excellent," Bill reiterated, as he prepared to leave. "It's the kind of thing the superintendent had in mind when he talked about leadership in the schools. I'll make sure he's aware of what's going on here!"

"Thanks," said Sissy. "I appreciate the feedback, as always!"

Sissy closed the door behind him and turned her attention to her last meeting of the day. She looked forward to meeting with the 2 + 2 committee. She felt what she had to say was anything but bad news for a change. Too often, meetings with individual teachers only happened when there was something unpleasant or awkward to discuss. Ideally, her plans to tame 2 + 2 even as she expanded the program in the name of professional development would be welcome news to the committee.

Joy, Andy, and Paige were in her office as soon as the last student had been dismissed. As they exchanged warm greetings, Joy realized how much their relationship had relaxed during the past six months. When they were all comfortable, Sissy began the meeting.

"I've been so pleased with all you've done, and I want you to know how much I appreciate your efforts. Because 2 + 2 has shown such interesting results, though, I've been doing a lot of thinking about the program. I wonder if 2 + 2, as successful as it is, could do more to live up to its potential. I know you're already planning some peer instruction in observation skills, so I'm no longer as concerned about the usefulness of the peer feedback. Some of the feedback I've seen has been really excellent. Looking at the big picture here at Dewey High, I have been concerned with how best to support teachers as we search for ways to make instruction more interdisciplinary, interactive, and relevant and also to make assessment more global. I can see, quite frankly, that saying it should happen doesn't make it so, even having had several workshops in these areas. Helping teachers improve what goes on in their classrooms is the bottom line. 2 + 2 gives everyone an opportunity to do that. I think the program would be of even greater benefit, though, if we tied our school and professional goals directly to 2 + 2 observations."

Joy was on the same wavelength and jumped right in. "I am glad to hear you say that," she said. "Couldn't we involve the whole faculty in developing a specific plan for the entire next year's staff development training days? After each inservice session, follow-up support would be provided through the use of 2 + 2 observations and feedback."

"That's not a bad idea," Sissy replied, pleased that Joy was also looking ahead. "Regarding our school improvement goals, we might enlarge the role faculty members have in developing them. From those goals, a number of observable components could be identified. For example, we won't just decide to count the number of interdisciplinary units being taught in the school. We can take it further by developing hallmarks of good interdisciplinary planning and teaching. Just for the sake of illustration, we could call cooperative learning a hallmark of an interdisciplinary approach. Then teachers can help each other by prioritizing their 2 + 2 feedback to consider if and how cooperative learning—or other hallmarks—are implemented in the classroom. Teachers who find they have special expertise in cooperative learning, or other areas, could hold voluntary mini inservice sessions for interested teachers. I suspect interest in such sessions would grow as teachers continue to learn to trust each other, much as has happened with the 2 + 2 process itself. I'm optimistic that this will be a great improvement over our usual one-day workshop approach to instruction."

"I like that idea a lot," said Andy. "I'm a little concerned, though, that observations will be required to have a predetermined focus. Couldn't we suggest a focus but leave the actual nature of the feedback up to the discretion of the teacher? That would leave some flexibility in the program."

"I could go along with that," replied Sissy. "But I would like to encourage teachers to align their observation focus with a previously agreed-on goal, unless they see another more pressing situation that requires feedback."

"I don't think that will be a problem," said Paige. "Most of the time, teachers do feel that having a narrower range of teaching behaviors to focus on helps them give better feedback."

"Getting back to school improvement," continued Joy, "we could do something similar with departmental programs. First, we can see how they're aligned with our school goals. Then we'll have to spend some time to establish, or reestablish, departmental priorities and formulate our areas of focus. I think it's important enough for departmental goals to be aligned, that the inservice time spent in this process will be well worth it. 2 + 2 observations could focus on departmental concerns as well, couldn't they?" she suggested. "Would it be possible to vary the focus of 2 + 2 observations, making adjustments as we agree on them? What do you think?" Joy asked the group.

"Well, as Dr. James pointed out to me, there are many variations of 2 + 2," Sissy responded. "Maybe he shared that with you, too, Joy. For example, teachers could pair up for peer coaching for a period of time; for the next six weeks, they could focus their observations on teachers in their own department. Later in the year, the emphasis might be on visiting as many teachers in different subject areas as possible. The point I am making is that any or all of those observations could have a common focus. That way, school improvement will start to be a coordinated and coherent process. But we won't forget individual needs, and exceptions to the rule are always possible."

"This sounds wonderful," Joy said. "I can't think of anything to add at the moment, except that we have a lot of planning ahead of us—which I'm definitely looking forward to. I've got something else on my mind, though. I wanted to raise the issue of performance appraisals. That came up when we first began experimenting with 2 + 2—do you remember? I included the feedback from teachers about the possibility of 2 + 2 replacing the performance appraisal system in my written proposal last semester. I don't think you've ever said anything in response to that. Any chance something can be done?" she asked hesitantly.

"I guess that issue has slipped my mind," Sissy replied. "I admit, earlier in the year I didn't want to consider 2 + 2 as an alternative to our district performance appraisal system. I thought it wasn't nearly rigorous enough. Raising the question again is not a bad idea. My definition of *rigor* has undergone some change since we last talked. I'm looking more closely at results—at evidence of improvement. On that score, I believe 2 + 2 is truly a viable alternative to our system.

"What I can do," she continued, "is request a waiver from the district and pilot the change here at Dewey High. I think I know someone downtown who could help me with that."

"That's wonderful," exclaimed Joy, Paige, and Andy at once.

They were beginning to get very excited at the collaborative work to be done. Sissy's ideas seemed to dovetail perfectly with their feedback from the teachers. They were amazed that here it was May, the busiest time of the year, and they were eagerly anticipating more planning for Dewey High's professional development program. "I think we'll get somewhere with this approach," Joy responded with enthusiasm. "I believe there's a good chance to make continuous improvement this way."

Sissy was not completely surprised. She was getting to know her teachers better. "I am pleased that we seem to have come to similar conclusions about the direction of the 2 + 2 program. I should have known you were coming up with wonderful ideas yourselves."

Joy paused, then added, "We may even want to invite parents in at some point, both to make sure what we're doing makes sense to them and to get their feedback."

"I think that would probably be reasonable, Joy," replied Sissy. "Feedback from parents is nearly nonexistent at the high school. We really do have our work cut out for us, don't we?"

"Speaking of feedback," said Andy, "we've been wondering how you would feel about receiving 2 + 2 feedback."

Sissy had somehow known that was coming. But she knew the kind of school climate she

> When conditions are right, 2 + 2 can replace older, more conventional performance appraisal systems.

wanted to cultivate, and she found herself curious to discover how her faculty viewed her. "Sure," she said, "that's all part of 2 + 2."

The last meeting of 2 + 2 teachers in June involved virtually the entire faculty. Instead of sharing their 2 + 2 experiences, though, teachers were still talking about the developments that occurred on the last staff inservice day. A discussion had taken place about the possibility of 2 + 2 serving as an alternative to the district performance appraisal system for those teachers wishing this option. Sissy agreed this was a good idea, with the condition that participation be subject to administrative approval. This would be a simple formality, she had assured them. But it would allow her to retain any marginal teacher on the district system. Virtually every teacher applauded this development. Sissy said that the alternative 2 + 2 performance appraisal program depended on a district waiver but that she was confident her upcoming meeting with the superintendent would go well. He had already agreed to the idea in principle. Now they just needed to formalize it in writing.

Teachers were nearly as excited about having a large role in Sissy's staff development strategy. Some teachers had even volunteered to spend time during the summer researching and fine-tuning different aspects of the upcoming professional development initiative. Sissy thought they should be paid for their work and was looking into possible stipends for them. She believed she had a good chance of success.

Joy had some interesting data as a result of her survey. Since more than 75% of the faculty had participated in some way in 2 + 2, and nearly everyone had responded, she could report her findings with some confidence. No one seemed surprised as she passed around a synopsis of the results.

The meeting lasted exactly one hour, and the refreshments had disappeared. Not much was discussed that specifically had to do with 2 + 2. Yet 2 + 2 had everything to do with the marked change in teachers' attitudes and in the direction of school improvement. The mood reflected the hectic atmosphere of the last days of school but was charged with a refreshing energy and optimism. Afterward, amid loud conversation and laughter, everyone dispersed quickly because final exams were waiting to be graded.

Joy, Paige, and Andy, though, paused to reflect on the year. "What a difference in the way I feel this year," began Andy. "I'm almost ready for next fall, and we haven't even finished out the year."

"Not me," laughed Paige, "but I do feel we've come a long way. I can't believe how many more teachers I have come to know—and to

Survey

Statement	% Agreeing
1. As a result of 2 + 2 participation, I have experimented with new instructional strategies.	84%
2. During 2 + 2 observations, I have seen strategies I wanted to try with my own students.	87%
3. More training would make 2 + 2 feedback more useful.	57%
4. I have implemented at least one 2 + 2 suggestion.	96%
5. I have implemented strategies I observed in other classrooms.	85%
6. 2 + 2 observations have helped me gain perspective on my own teaching abilities.	83%
7. The 2 + 2 program has helped me gain confidence as a teacher.	65%
8. The quality of interaction among my colleagues has improved as a result of 2 + 2.	72%
9. 2 + 2 has had no impact on my professional growth.	7%

NOTE: This survey represents actual data from a participating 2 + 2 school.

respect. And I really think I'm a better teacher than I was at this time last year. At least I have a much better idea of where I stand and where I want to be heading."

"I know what you mean," said Joy. "I was even considering leaving teaching last year. I couldn't figure out what was wrong. Now that we're working together on ways to improve, I do have a sense of hope and optimism. Thanks to both of you, 2 + 2 has come to be more than I imagined last summer. Sissy has really changed her agenda, too. I think she's figuring out how to give teachers encouragement and support where they need it—in the classroom. That's the most important thing. But I'm also beginning to see how my classroom is a part of the whole school picture, too. And now we have the chance to determine how that larger picture looks. I think we're all going to have an interesting year."

Sissy, who had just walked in, overheard them. "Thanks for the compliment," she said. "We all do best working together and with plenty of encouragement! Thank you, too, for your support and initiative. I'm really looking forward to next year."

As they returned to their respective duties, they were all satisfied that they had discovered a mechanism for supporting the staff and improving the quality of everyone's teaching. A sense of hope and joy permeated Dewey High.

Epilogue

Two Years Later

B ill, who was now the district superintendent, sat in his office reviewing his last visit to Dewey High School. Sissy had been appointed assistant superintendent for curriculum and instruction, but she was still serving as principal until the school year was over. That had been her choice. She had wanted to be a part of the exciting changes at Dewey High for as long as possible.

What had changed? The 2 + 2 Alternative Performance Appraisal Program was now thriving. Certain formal requirements were in place, of course. The reflection reports became part of a teacher's permanent record, and each teacher was responsible for a minimum number of observations. Administrator feedback was an integral part of the program, including administrative comment on the teachers' 2 + 2 portfolios.

> The culture of 2 + 2 can make feedback and encouragement the foundation of every aspect of school life.

Student feedback was an accepted part of the appraisal process. Amazingly, performance appraisal was an ongoing, annual process, no longer relegated to an exercise once every three years. That decision had met with full faculty consent.

Bill smiled. He was looking forward to revamping the appraisal system for the entire district along the lines of the Dewey High program.

Beyond the formal requirements of the appraisal process, the practice of giving compliments and suggestions was simply a part of everyday interactions at the school. Teachers, for example, frequently wrote quick 2 + 2s on faculty meetings or administrative actions. Parents were encouraged to note compliments and suggestions after parent-teacher conferences, meetings with administrators, or PTA meetings. Gradually, they were taking advantage of the feedback process. Bill suspected it was because the Dewey High staff truly wanted their feedback. For instance, at the suggestion of a parent, teachers began to hold conferences in the different neighborhoods where students lived. Sissy reported a steady increase in parent participation in these conferences over time. Compared with two years ago, in fact, parent participation in conferences, school events, and meetings had tripled.

Teachers had suggested funding several colleagues' attendance at workshops during the school year so that the information could later be shared with the entire staff. The climate at Dewey High was so collaborative that the ensuing school-based workshops enjoyed nearly 100% attendance. 2 + 2 visits provided follow-up for new ideas introduced at the workshops. Improvement in the level of teaching had been the result so far.

Teachers were taking on more leadership roles. Joy, Andy, Paige, and several other teachers were occasionally released from classroom duties to coach other schools in adopting a 2 + 2 program. The district paid for this initiative.

Joy was scheduled to move into a new role as the assistant principal of another district high school next fall. Bill had wanted her to move to the district office's staff development department. Joy, however, felt it would be much more exciting to remain at the school level and see how she could encourage change where it counted most—in the classroom. Bill was confident that she would quickly learn to lead a school and hoped to soon move her into a principalship. She already had some practice, having brought 2 + 2 to the Greendale School District. He would ask Sissy to serve as her mentor.

Bill was especially pleased to note that classroom, departmental, and school goals and improvement efforts were aligned. Communication and feedback were paying off in a big way. Student performance had increased on all measures at Dewey High, compared with two years prior. Was 2 + 2 responsible for that? Bill couldn't say. But he was quite certain Dewey High was a better place because of it. So many things had changed since 2 + 2 was first introduced—almost all of them directly traceable to that initial 2 + 2 implementation.

Needless to say, relations between the administration and the staff were at an all-time high. Trust had grown through the 2 + 2 implementation, and, of course, the 2 + 2 program had matured as a result of increased trust. Excellent relations between teachers were reflected in the large number of collaborative projects that were always in progress at the high school. Staff and students alike seemed to enjoy being at Dewey High. Morale was simply great.

Incredible, Bill thought, *that so much change and improvement can happen in two years.* The power of feedback and encouragement could not be underestimated. The thought brought him much satisfaction—and joy.

2 + 2 for Teachers

Frequently
Asked Questions

Teaching is a profession that isolates professionals from one another without intending to do so. The result is that very little opportunity exists for teachers to gain the benefit of multiple perspectives on their professional practice. To compound the problem, classroom observation has a decidedly negative connotation, mixed with images of evaluation, supervision, assessment, accountability, threat, and comparison. Suggestions for improvement are often incidental to the process, sometimes missing entirely. The 2 + 2 for teachers model counteracts conditions that result in teacher isolation and fosters the growth of a learning community among teachers in a way that can be customized according to a school's needs and that is cost-neutral.

What Is 2 + 2 for Teachers?

2 + 2 for teachers is a concept of classroom observation that focuses on the power of feedback, encouragement, discussion and discourse, and the importance of perspective and collaboration in the improvement of instruction. In a 2 + 2 observation, the observer, trained or untrained, is asked to observe a classroom for as long as necessary to identify two compliments and two suggestions for improvement. Focused feedback provides the optimal environment for constructive dialogue and improvement. The concept is simple. All lessons have potential for constructive suggestions for improvement, and no lesson is totally devoid of merit. We all appreciate

compliments or recognition of our strengths and accomplishments. Such appreciation helps us become more open to suggestions for improvement.

In the 2 + 2 model, everyone understands from the outset that each classroom visit will be followed by two compliments and two suggestions from the observer in writing. One significant result of such an arrangement is that educators are able to focus on strengths (compliments) and weaknesses (suggestions) without the stigma attached to recommendations under current systems. Suggestions for improvement are seen as a beneficial part of the total observation process. The emphasis is placed on the tenet that a person does not have to be sick to get better. Especially in implementations where 2 + 2 for teachers replaces the traditional performance appraisal system, this new approach ultimately frees both teachers and administrators to focus on strengths and weaknesses while eliminating the adversarial dynamics that all too often arise from more traditional methods of evaluation. However, similar changes in climate and attitude can also be anticipated where 2 + 2 is used as a supplement to the traditional performance appraisal program.

As educators engage in 2 + 2, teacher isolation is alleviated through regular peer observation and resultant discussions about teaching and learning. Such a situation provides a remarkable contrast to many current methods, which largely discourage open and frank discussion of performance among colleagues.

In the 2 + 2 model, no rating or comparison is required or desired. Success comes from a mutual recognition of strengths and the offer of suggestions that, at the teacher's discretion, can be successfully implemented, considered and rejected, or identified as agendas for future development. Powerful and authentic assessment can grow out of continued 2 + 2 observations but only after the agreement of all parties to use them for such purposes.

What Happens During a 2 + 2 Observation?

Observers visit another teacher's classroom, usually without prior notice. A visit may take place at any time during a class period. The observer takes a seat and observes for as long as it takes to formulate two compliments and two suggestions, usually ten to fifteen minutes. The written comments are left with the teacher or are written later and given to the teacher by the end of the day. It is helpful to have

2 + 2 observation forms available in duplicate so that both the observer and the teacher observed can keep copies of the feedback in their 2 + 2 portfolios for later reference.

Who Are the 2 + 2 Observers?

The essence of 2 + 2 for teachers is peer observation. It is as important and beneficial for teachers to have the opportunity to see other teachers teach as it is for those being observed to receive compliments and suggestions from their peers. In most implementations, administrators are also active observers, documenting their comments on 2 + 2 observation forms. Besides providing valuable feedback, active administrative participation shows support for the program.

In addition to teachers and administrators, student teachers, parents, and students are all potential observers. Feedback from students, for example, can be very useful. Teachers could arrange with students in one or more classes to have a different student each day complete a 2 + 2 observation. Or an entire class can write 2 + 2 feedback, and the teacher might skim the comments, highlighting those that are useful and discarding the rest. The quality of compliments and suggestions from students will be quite varied, but student perception, even inaccurate perception, can be valuable to the teacher in planning instructional strategies. Even if students are misguided in their perceptions, teachers are well served to know what they think. A parallel objective is for students' confidence in the educational process to increase as they are asked to become actively involved in providing feedback. However, compliments and suggestions are provided for the benefit of the teacher, and the teacher alone retains the right to judge when comments are useful and when they are to be discarded.

Does There Need to Be a Conference After a 2 + 2 Observation?

Post-observation conferences are not a requirement of 2 + 2. Teachers are encouraged, however, to discuss any questions resulting from 2 + 2 observations or feedback. In practice, many teachers naturally discuss 2 + 2 observations informally when they see each other. Even brief encounters in school halls are useful for such exchanges.

Can 2 + 2 Be Implemented in Conjunction With a Traditional Performance Appraisal System?

Yes. The 2 + 2 program is flexible and beneficial in most any context. It may be possible to link participation in 2 + 2 with recertification points. 2 + 2 participation may also enhance a teacher's traditional performance appraisal by allowing the teacher to exceed the performance appraisal standard in a given domain, such as professional development.

Can 2 + 2 Be Used to Replace the Traditional Performance Appraisal System?

Yes. For the large majority of teachers, 2 + 2 provides an exceptional opportunity for sustained professional growth. Typical objectives of traditional performance appraisal systems are subsumed in 2 + 2. These include objectives such as "recognizing professional strengths," "helping effect the transition of curriculum development and the acquisition of new instructional strategies into the classroom," or "encouraging creativity, innovation, and leadership." Participation in lieu of a traditional performance appraisal system would usually be subject to administrator approval. A school may create a 2 + 2 contract stating the number of observations the teacher is expected to make and other stipulations, such as the maintenance of a portfolio or submission of a reflection report. An endorsement by an administrator that the contract has been satisfactorily fulfilled completes the appraisal process. A conference to discuss the 2 + 2 experience may be used for the endorsement process. Summative ratings or comparisons are neither necessary nor desirable.

What if an Administrator Has Serious Concerns About a Teacher's Performance After Approving Participation in 2 + 2?

When an administrator has serious concerns about a teacher's performance that cannot be addressed by the 2 + 2 process, the administrator may remove the teacher from the 2 + 2 program. The teacher is then placed in the district's performance appraisal system for further administrative action. Removal from 2 + 2 due to the administration's concern can occur at any time during the year. Documentation of a teacher's poor performance for use with the district's appraisal system, however, should begin only after a teacher is removed from 2 + 2. This allows teachers to remain confident that as long as they are 2 + 2 participants their status is not in question.

Should Participation in the 2 + 2 Program Be Voluntary?

Yes. Mandating 2 + 2 without sufficient preparatory participation on a voluntary basis (several years) may significantly change the dynamics of self-discovery and trust. Administrative support is vital for success. Teachers must know that administrators value the process and take it seriously before they will commit to participate. Administrative support can also allay fears that the process is risky or threatening.

How Many Observations Should Teachers Conduct Each Semester?

The number of observations may vary according to time constraints and other considerations unique to each school. A minimum of ten observations per semester, however, is a good guideline. Fewer observations may significantly dilute the benefits of the program.

What if a Teacher Conducts the Agreed-on Number of Observations but Has Too Few Teachers Observe His or Her Classroom?

This situation may occur because of schedule conflicts and the likelihood that observations will not be evenly distributed among all teachers on the basis of chance alone. For this reason, a mechanism for achieving an overview of observation activity is useful. The mechanism may take the form of a sign-up sheet, on which teachers sign up to visit a colleague as long as the agreed-on number of observations is not reached. When a teacher has the required number of observers signed up, an observer would need to choose another teacher to observe.

Another form of self-regulation would involve posting a list of participating teachers in a central location. After an observation, the teacher who made the observation would place a checkmark next to the observed teacher's name. Teachers could consult the list when planning their observations and choose to visit those teachers with fewer check marks.

A school may, of course, develop other means to ensure that all teachers receive adequate observations and feedback.

How Can Teachers Overcome Difficulties Making Suggestions? How Can They Improve the Quality of Their Suggestions?

Certain factors sometimes make 2 + 2 suggestions difficult to formulate. One factor is the hesitation teachers may feel to point out an area for improvement to their colleagues. A second factor is the inexperience of teachers in identifying specific areas of the teaching act and making focused comments.

The first issue involves an element of trust. An orientation session may help establish the premise that 2 + 2 involves two compliments and two suggestions. Everyone is expected to give and receive this combination of feedback.

In addressing the second issue, teachers have found the following to be helpful in learning to make specific, focused comments:

- A list of teaching performance categories to help focus their comments
- Informal meetings with 2 + 2 colleagues to discuss their experiences with the process
- Sample suggestions or access to suggestions made by other teachers
- Informal sessions with colleagues who have had some supervisory or peer observation experience

Suggestions may also be framed as an alternative strategy or idea. Even a very good lesson may be taught in more than one way. A suggestion for an alternative way to teach a concept does not mean the method used by the teacher was wrong.

Constructive criticism can be formulated with tact. Teachers may find it useful to preface comments with phrases such as "You may have already thought of this, but what about . . ." or "I sometimes find it very useful to . . . when my students are acting up."

What About Suggestions That a Teacher Feels Are Irrelevant or Are Based on a Misunderstanding of the Classroom Situation?

Some feedback will inevitably miss the mark. The teacher is responsible for determining the usefulness of 2 + 2 feedback. Feedback that is not relevant or useful, from whatever the source, may be ignored. Experience has shown that teachers are sometimes irritated with feedback that addresses issues not under their control. Teachers should take care not to personalize situations where feedback seems based on these or similar misunderstandings.

Who Will See the 2 + 2 Feedback?

In addition to the observer and the teacher being observed, who sees the feedback depends on prior agreement. If 2 + 2 is an informal supplement to the official performance appraisal system, the agreement may be that the teacher chooses whether or not to share feedback with his or her administrator.

When 2 + 2 replaces the traditional performance appraisal system, the feedback is part of the formal assessment. In some cases, the agreement may be that the administration receives a copy of each observation feedback form. In other cases, the agreement may be that only the reflection report is shared and discussed with an administrator.

Ultimately, teachers' 2 + 2 portfolios might be open for any colleague or administrator to view. Observers would then have an option to make comments with reference to prior feedback. For example, a teacher may have implemented a prior suggestion. The observer might note that fact in the current observation in the compliments section.

Trust is key. Every 2 + 2 teacher should be aware that feedback will sometimes be inaccurate and that no lesson is perfect. Generally, feelings of self-consciousness disappear quickly.

What Is a 2 + 2 Portfolio?

Teachers maintain all relevant 2 + 2 materials in a 2 + 2 portfolio. The 2 + 2 portfolio contains forms from observations the teacher has received as well as copies of forms from observations the teacher has made. The portfolio is useful for reviewing feedback received, noting actions taken with regard to particular suggestions (these notes may be made on the form in the reflections section), and monitoring the type and quality of suggestions made to colleagues. The portfolio is the basis for the reflection report, usually submitted at the close of each semester.

What Is a Reflection Report?

A reflection report is the teacher's own written reflections on the feedback given and received. It is usually submitted to the school administration at the close of each semester. The reflection report provides a structure and process that teachers use to reflect on their 2 + 2 experience. A typical reflection report may entail completion of the following process:

1. Teachers review their 2 + 2 portfolio and determine which ten compliments and ten suggestions were of most value to them.

2. Teachers then choose several of the most useful compliments and suggestions and discuss how their classroom teaching routines were affected. The impact of observing other teachers is likewise reflected on. Any future plans for classroom experimentation or implementation that have emerged from the 2 + 2 process are also discussed. Teachers are thus empowered to determine what they learn and to give credit to their peers for excellent compliments and suggestions.

3. The completed reflection reports are submitted to the administration for review, generally with the teacher present.

4. When the administrator is in agreement that the report reflects the growth of the teacher, the administrator endorses the reflection report, and it becomes part of the teacher's permanent record.

The number of compliments and suggestions to reflect in the reflection report may be established by each school. Ten compliments and suggestions is a number that has worked well in actual 2 + 2 implementation.

How Does the 2 + 2 Program Support Staff Development Needs?

The 2 + 2 program can provide systematic, frequent follow-up for a school's staff development program. For example, teachers might form small self-study groups whose members regularly observe each other and meet for discussion. The observation feedback would be focused on a particular staff development agenda supporting existing school improvement efforts, interdisciplinary thematic approaches, or teaming initiatives. Different self-study groups might focus on different initiatives. Self-study groups might also form to plan lessons collaboratively and observe lesson implementation. Teachers are encouraged to determine pertinent areas of focus for staff development purposes as a result of their observations or in response to their school's needs.

With the specific focus of an observation agreed on beforehand, observers can specifically address these areas in their compliments and suggestions. (Observers may also be told, however, that they should feel free to ignore such areas of focus if other more compelling issues are noted during an observation.) In this way, the repertoire of potential areas for suggestions and compliments will be tied to specific staff development priorities.

Workshops and training sessions could be developed for specific areas of focus or teaching skills. While external experts may be invited to conduct such sessions, the teachers' own self-study groups are also valuable resources for full or partial staff workshops.

Index

**CORWIN
PRESS**

The Corwin Press logo—a raven striding across an open book—represents the union of courage and learning. Corwin Press is committed to improving education for all learners by publishing books and other professional development resources for those serving the field of K–12 education. By providing practical, hands-on materials, Corwin Press continues to carry out the promise of its motto: **"Helping Educators Do Their Work Better."**